Dictionary of Antonyms and Near Antonyms

DR. REGY JOSEPH

INDIA • SINGAPORE • MALAYSIA

Notion Press

Old No. 38, New No. 6
McNichols Road, Chetpet
Chennai - 600 031

First Published by Notion Press 2019
Copyright © Dr. Regy Joseph 2019
All Rights Reserved.

ISBN 978-1-64587-149-1

A

Abandon	x	Retain, claim, keep.
Abase	x	Honour, elevate, rise.
Abash	x	Appease, comfort, encourage.
Abate	x	Aggravate, enhance, amplify.
Abatement	x	Augmentation, increase, enlargement.
Abbreviate	x	Expand, lengthen, stretch.
Abbreviation	x	Expansion, amplification, expatiation.
Abdicate	x	Claim, accept, occupy.
Abduct	x	Restore, reinstate, adduct.
Aberrant	x	Normal, regular, natural.
Abet	x	Deter, hinder, impede.
Abeyance	x	Renewal, revival, resuscitation.
Abhor	x	Adore, like, approve.

Abhorrent	x	Desirable, admirable, enjoyable.
Abide	x	Abandon, shun, resist.
Ability	x	Inability, disability, incapacity.
Able	x	Unable, unfit, disinclined.
Able	x	Unable, incapable, powerless.
Abnegation	x	Assertion, vindication, proposal.
Abnormal	x	Normal, ordinary, common.
Abolish	x	Retain, establish, promote.
Abominable	x	Admirable, acceptable, attractive.
Aboriginal	x	Immigrant, subsequent, recent.
Abortion	x	Consummation, completion, development.
Abound	x	Lack, lessen, waste.
About	x	Exactly, precisely, afar.
Above	x	Below, beneath, lower.
Aboveboard	x	Bogus, underhand, secretly.
Abreast	x	Ahead, astern, behind.
Abridge	x	Enlarge, expand, amplify.
Abrogate	x	Enact, enforce, establish.

Abrupt	x	Gradual, expected, easy.
Abscond	x	Show, appear, emerge.
Absence	x	Presence, awareness, existence.
Absolute	x	Conditional, provisional, limited.
Absolve	x	Accuse, convict, charge.
Absorb	x	Exude, eject, radiate.
Abstain	x	Indulge, gratify, yield to.
Abstemious	x	Unrestrained, sensual, greedy.
Abstract	x	Concrete, expansion, amplification.
Abstruse	x	Clear, concrete, superficial.
Absurd	x	Reasonable, sensible, substantial.
Abundance	x	Scarcity, dearth, deficiency.
Abundant	x	Scarce, rare, drained.
Abuse	x	Honour, protect, praise.
Abut	x	Diverge, recede, return.
Accede	x	Reject, decline, refuse.
Accelerate	x	Slow down, delay, obstruct.
Accept	x	Reject, refuse, disown.

Acceptable	x	Unacceptable, rejection, exclusion.
Accession	x	Abandonment, decrease, resignation.
Accidental	x	Deliberate, intended, purposed.
Accommodate	x	Deprive, dislodge, disturb.
Accompany	x	Abandon, discard, desert.
Accomplice	x	Rival, enemy, adversary.
Accomplish	x	Fail, spoil, defeat.
Accomplishment	x	Failure, blunder, folly.
Accord	x	Discord, differ, deny.
Accost	x	Depart, rebuff, ignore.
Account	x	Underrate, undervalue, disesteem.
Accountable	x	Independent, absolute, autocratic.
Accredit	x	Credit, dismiss, discard.
Accredited	x	Unauthorised, distrusted, discredited.
Accretion	x	Erosion, abrasion, diminution.
Accrue	x	Dwindle, reduce, weaken.
Accumulate	x	Disburse, separate, dissipate.
Accuracy	x	Inaccuracy, error, fallacy.

Accurate	x	Inaccurate, defective, careless.
Accuse	x	Discharge, acquit, vindicate.
Accustom	x	Estrange, wean, alienate.
Ache	x	Pleasure, relief, delight.
Achieve	x	Fail, omit, lose.
Acknowledge	x	Deny, disclaim, ignore.
Acme	x	Nadir, base, foot.
Acquaintance	x	Stranger, ignorance, unfamiliarity.
Acquiesce	x	Resist, object, dissent.
Acquire	x	Lose, surrender, forfeit.
Acquit	x	Convict, charge, sentence.
Acrimony	x	Harmony, gentleness, courtesy.
Act	x	Rest, undo, neglect.
Action	x	Rest, passiveness, truce.
Active	x	Passive, dull, lazy.
Actual	x	Fictitious, virtual, hypothetical.
Acute	x	Dull, blunt, chronic.
Adaptation	x	Incompatibility, incongruity, misfit.

Add	x	Subtract, deduct, reduce.
Addicted	x	Averse, disinclined, unaccustomed.
Addition	x	Subtraction, decrease, diminution.
Address	x	Avoid, elude, ignore.
Adept	x	Inferior, useless, worthless.
Adequate	x	Inadequate, deficient, unfit.
Adhere	x	Part, separate, sever.
Adherence	x	Desertion, separation, disunion.
Adjacent	x	Distant, remote, detached.
Adjourn	x	Conclude, complete, consummate.
Adjunct	x	Detriment, impediment, obstruction.
Adjure	x	Defy, deprecate, expostulate.
Adjustment	x	Disturbance, dissension, divergence.
Administer	x	Withhold, retain, betray.
Admiration	x	Disapproval, contempt, dislike.
Admire	x	Despise, dislike, scorn.
Admire	x	Insult, blame, condemn.
Admissible	x	Absurd, preposterous, unlawful.

Admission	x	Denial, contradiction, rejection.
Admission	x	Denial, rejection, disclaimer.
Admit	x	Deny, exclude, reject.
Admonish	x	Encourage, urge, countenance.
Admonition	x	Applause, incitement, instigation.
Ado	x	Quiet, calm, composure.
Adopt	x	Abandon, reject, disown.
Adoration	x	Execration, disesteem, abomination.
Adore	x	Abhor, despise, hate.
Adorn	x	Mar, spoil, disfigure.
Adroit	x	Clumsy, awkward, maladroit.
Adulation	x	Defamation, obloquy, ridicule.
Advance	x	Retreat, hinder, withdraw.
Advantage	x	Disadvantage, loss, disappointment.
Advent	x	Departure, exit, exodus.
Adventitious	x	Intrinsic, pertinent, regular.
Adventurous	x	Timid, hesitating, cautious, cowardly.
Adversary	x	Ally, accomplice, abettor.

Adverse	x	Favorable, friendly, propitious.
Adversity	x	Prosperity, fortune, benefit.
Advertent	x	Thoughtless, inconsiderate, inattentive.
Advertise	x	Suppress, hush, conceal.
Advice	x	Restraint, expostulation, deception.
Advocate	x	Accuser, impugner, opponent.
Affable	x	Distant, unapproachable, inaccessible.
Affect	x	Shun, repel, repudiate.
Affectation	x	Simplicity, artlessness, genuineness.
Affection	x	Hatred, indifference, disaffection.
Affiance	x	Disloyalty, distrust, treason.
Affiliate	x	Sever, separate, dissociate.
Affinity	x	Repugnance, discordance, antipathy.
Affirm	x	Deny, doubt, contradict.
Affirmation	x	Doubt, denial, disapproval.
Affirmative	x	Negative, declination, denial.
Affix	x	Remove, detach, separate.
Affliction	x	Consolation, relief, gratification.

Affluence	x	Poverty, want, scarcity.
Affluent	x	Poor, un affluent, destitute.
Afford	x	Withhold, deny, retain.
Affray	x	Peace, amity, friendship.
Affront	x	Courtesy, amends, compliment.
Afire	x	Out, quenched, extinguished.
Afloat	x	Moored, anchored, stranded.
Aforesaid	x	Subsequent, forthcoming, below.
Afraid	x	Unafraid, fearless, secure.
After	x	Before, preceding, prior.
Again	x	Once, continuously, uninterruptedly.
Against	x	For, with, beside.
Agape	x	Listless, lukewarm, incurious, indifferent.
Agent	x	Counteragent, counter-actor, opponent.
Aggravate	x	Soothe, assuage, diminish.
Aggregation	x	Dispersion, dissipation, separation.

Aggression	x	Retaliation, repulsion, resistance.
Aghast	x	Cool, indifferent, unaffected.
Agile	x	Heavy, clumsy, awkward.
Agitate	x	Calm, allay, pacify.
Ago	x	Future, hereafter, hence.
Agony	x	Ecstasy, assuagement, comfort.
Agree	x	Disagree, deny, differ.
Agreeable	x	Disagreeable, unpleasant, offensive.
Agreement	x	Disagreement, discord, denial.
Aground	x	Afloat, loose, abroad.
Ahead	x	Abaft, astern, behind.
Aid	x	Oppose, discourage, deter.
Aided	x	Unaided, unassisted, discouraged.
Ailing	x	Healthy, energetic, strong.
Ailment	x	Health, vigor, recovery.
Aim	x	Aimless, deviation, divergence.
Airy	x	Un-airy, low, depressed.
Akin	x	Foreign, alien, hostile.

Alacrity	x	Reluctance, aversion, refusal.
Alarm	x	Confidence, quiet, composure.
Alert	x	Inert, slow, sluggish.
Alien	x	Native, citizen, countryman.
Alienation	x	Confederacy, coalition, Union.
Alight	x	Board, ascend, mount.
Alike	x	Different, unequal, distinct.
Alive	x	Dead, defunct, lifeless.
All	x	Part, some, portion.
Allay	x	Enemy, harm hurt.
Allege	x	Contradict, deny, abandon.
Allegiance	x	Treason, rebellion, disloyalty.
Allegory	x	Fact, narrative, record.
Alleviate	x	Augment, increase, intensify.
Alliance	x	Separation, estrangement, divorce.
Allies	x	Enemies, detractors, opponents.
Allot	x	Refuse, retain, confiscate.
Allow	x	Disallow, forbid, refuse.

Allowance	x	Refusal, disapproval, denial.
Alloy	x	Genuineness, enhancement, purity.
Allude	x	Demonstrate, specify, declare.
Allure	x	Dissuade, repel, warn.
Allusion	x	Mention, demonstration, specification.
Ally	x	Opponent, adversary, enemy.
Aloft	x	Beneath, earthward, below.
Alone	x	Together, accompanied, associated.
Along	x	Across, sidewise lateral.
Aloof	x	Close, together, united.
Aloud	x	Softly, silently, inaudibly.
Also	x	Contrarily, dissimilarly, otherwise.
Alter	x	Retain, conserve, preserve.
Alteration	x	Changelessness, fixity, permanence.
Altercation	x	Concord, compromise, reconciliation.
Altered	x	Unaltered, fixed, dateless.
Alternate	x	Continuous, successive, consequent.
Alternative	x	Compulsion, quandary, fixity.

Altitude	x	Depth, declivity, descent.
Altogether	x	Partially, partly, separately.
Altruism	x	Egoism, selfishness, meanness.
Always	x	Never, now, occasionally.
Amalgamate	x	Disintegrate, decompose, separate.
Amass	x	Disperse, divide, spend.
Amateur	x	Professional, expert, licensed.
Amazing	x	Common, trivial, frequent.
Ambiguous	x	Clear, plain, direct, straight.
Ambition	x	Contentment, moderation, indifference.
Amelioration	x	Degeneration, deterioration, detriment.
Amenable	x	Obstinate, irresponsible, independent.
Amend	x	Harm, corrupt, aggravate.
Amends	x	Insult, injury, fault.
Amenity	x	Austerity, ungraciousness, discourtesy.
Amiable	x	Cruel, Crusty, hateful.
Amicable	x	Unkind, distant, hostile.

Amid	x	Outside, without, beyond.
Amiss	x	Correct, perfect, effective.
Ample	x	Niggardly, stingy, scant.
Amplify	x	Simplify, condense, abridge.
Amusement	x	Weariness, disgust, monotony.
Anabolism	x	catabolism, metabolism, dissimilation.
Analogy	x	Unlikeness, incongruity, disproportion.
Analysis	x	Synthesis, composition, combination.
Anarchy	x	Order, control, organization.
Anatomy	x	Synthesis, organization, construction.
Ancient	x	Modern, fresh, new.
Ancillary	x	Alien, adverse, obstructive.
Angelic	x	Demoniac, diabolical, hellish.
Anger	x	Patience, forbearance, mildness.
Angry	x	Pleased, calm, self-controlled.
Anguish	x	Ease, relief, solace.
Animate	x	Inanimate, lifeless, dead.
Animosity	x	Congeniality, unanimity, harmony.

Annals	x	Tradition, hearsay, legend.
Annex	x	Separate, detach, remove.
Annihilation	x	Perpetuation, immortality, genesis.
Annotation	x	Narrative, text, assert.
Announce	x	Suppress, conceal, withhold.
Announcement	x	Suppression, concealment, secrecy.
Annoyance	x	Delight, ease, pleasure.
Annul	x	Conserve, confirm, establish.
Anomalous	x	Normal, regular, common.
Anon	x	Herewith, now, already.
Anonymous	x	Authorized, authenticated, attested.
Answer	x	Question, interrogate, query.
Answerable	x	Independent, irresponsible, irrefutable.
Antagonism	x	Amity, alliance, association.
Antecedent	x	Subsequent, posterior, following.
Antedate	x	Postdate, follow, succeed.
Anticipate	x	Recall, recollect, dread.
Anticipation	x	Realization, despair, surprise.

Antipathy	x	Sympathy, attraction, affinity.
Antiquated	x	Modern, recent, fashionable.
Antiquity	x	Modernity, futurity, the present.
Antonym	x	Synonym, same, similar.
Anxiety	x	Confidence, ease, contentment.
Any	x	Many, all, neither.
Apathy	x	Fury, susceptibility, sensitiveness.
Ape	x	Vary, modify, change.
Aperture	x	Closure, seclusion, imperviousness.
Apex	x	Base, bottom, minimum.
Apex	x	Base, foot, root.
Aphorism	x	Lecture, disquisition, discourse.
Apiece	x	Together, collectively, synthetically.
Apocryphal	x	Palpable, authorized, authentic, verified.
Apology	x	Complaint, offense, insult.
Apostate	x	Adherent, supporter, fanatic.
Apothegm	x	Sermon, discourse, tirade.
Appall	x	Reassure, charm, tempt.

Apparel	x	Nudity, rags, tatters.
Apparent	x	Hidden, dubious, doubtful.
Appeal	x	Protest, defy, abjure.
Appearance	x	Disappearance, departure, vanishing.
Appease	x	Aggravate, provoke, inflame.
Appendage	x	Main body, whole, total.
Appetite	x	Aversion, loathing, disgust.
Applause	x	Denunciation, censure, blame.
Applicable	x	Irrelevant, useless, impertinent.
Apply	x	Divert, misuse, discard.
Appoint	x	Dismiss, cancel, suspend.
Apportion	x	Retain, collect, receive.
Apposite	x	Untimely, irrelevant, impertinent.
Appraise	x	Undervalue, discard, discount.
Appreciate	x	Depreciate, undervalue, ignore.
Apprehend	x	Miss, ignore, misconceive.
Apprehension	x	Misapprehension, escape, lethargy.
Apprise	x	Deceive, mislead, hood wink.

Approach	x	Diverge, retreat, restrain.
Approbation	x	Censure, protest, dissatisfaction.
Appropriate	x	Inappropriate, improper, incorrect.
Approve	x	Disapprove, condemn, disown.
Approximation	x	Remoteness, variation, divergence.
A priori	x	A posteriori, practically, deductively from facts.
Apropos	x	Inopportune, irrelevant, unsuitable.
Apt	x	Irrelevant, improper, averse.
Aptitude	x	Dislike, antipathy, repugnance.
Arbiter	x	Appellant, claimant, litigant.
Arbitrary	x	Logical, Considerate, lenient.
Arbitration	x	Litigation, contention, appeal.
Ardent	x	Halfhearted, Cool, indifferent.
Ardor	x	Indifference, apathy, detachment.
Arduous	x	Easy, accessible, effortless.
Argue	x	Agree, accept, concur.
Argument	x	Assertion, assumption, dogma.
Arid	x	Fertile, damp, humid.

Aridity	x	Humidity, Moisture, damp.
Arise	x	Decline, descend, fall.
Aristocrat	x	Commoner, peasant, boor.
Arm	x	Disarm, divest, expose.
Armed	x	Unarmed, armless, defenseless.
Aromatic	x	Odorless, scentless, malodorous.
Arouse	x	Allay, mitigate, quell.
Arraign	x	Acquit, discharge, release.
Arrange	x	Dearrange, jumble, disorder.
Array	x	Disarray, confusion, jumble.
Arrest	x	Release, free, discharge.
Arrival	x	Departure, leave, exist.
Arrive	x	Depart, set out, gone.
Arrogance	x	Modesty, humility, confusion.
Arrogant	x	Humble, diffident, polite.
Artful	x	Artless, guileless, innocent.
Articulate	x	Inarticulate, disperse, separate.
Artifice	x	Fairness, frankness, sincerity.

Artificial	x	Natural, real, genuine.
Ascend	x	Descend, fall, sink.
Ascendancy	x	Subordination, servility, disadvantage.
Ascertain	x	Guess, surmise, suppose.
Ascetic	x	Hedonistic, lenient, indulgent.
Ascribe	x	Dissociate, exclude, deny.
Ask	x	Answer, command, claim.
Asperity	x	Softness, gentleness, mildness.
Aspiration	x	Apathy, inertia, indifference.
Assault	x	Defense, resistance, retaliation.
Assemble	x	Disperse, scatter, dismiss.
Assembly	x	Dispersion, dismissal, disruption.
Assent	x	Dissent, disagreement, difference.
Assert	x	Dispute, disregard, deny.
Assertion	x	Denial, contradiction, protest.
Assiduous	x	Lazy, indolent, desultory.
Assignment	x	Withdrawal, refusal, rejection.
Assimilate	x	Reject, contrast, segregate.

Assist	x	Hinder, oppose, resist.
Associate	x	Dissociate, enemy, opponent.
Association	x	Dissociation, solitude, independence.
Assortment	x	Disarrangement, displacement, misplacement.
Assuage	x	Excite, inflame, provoke.
Assume	x	Unassuming, prove, argue.
Assumption	x	Truth, fact, distrust.
Assurance	x	Doubt, distrust, confusion.
Astonish	x	Encourage, embolden, assure.
Astute	x	Stupid, dull, idiotic, shallow.
Atheism	x	Theism, belief, trust.
Atom	x	Mass, lot, chunk.
Atrocious	x	Mild, noble, admirable.
Attachment	x	Detachment, alienation, aversion.
Attack	x	Defend, resist, support.
Attain	x	Lose, forfeit, abandon.
Attainment	x	Inspiration, intuition, ignorance.
Attempt	x	Abandon, shun, neglect.

Attendance	x	Absence, non-attendance, neglect.
Attention	x	Inattention, indifference, distraction.
Attenuate	x	Intensify, amplify, expand.
Attest	x	Refute, controvert, contradict.
Attire	x	Nudity, nakedness, undress.
Attitude	x	State, condition, essence.
Attract	x	Repel, deter, disgust.
Attraction	x	Repulsion, aversion, repugnance.
Attractive	x	Unattractive, boring, repellent.
Attribute	x	Separate, disconnect, dissociate.
Audacious	x	Polite, cowardly, cautious.
Audacity	x	Timidity, modesty, diffidence.
Audible	x	Inaudible, silent, voiceless.
August	x	Humble, mean, paltry.
Auspicious	x	Inauspicious, hopeless, unpromising.
Austere	x	Affable, genial, tender.
Authentic	x	Counterfeit, fake, spurious.
Author	x	Destroyer, demolisher, spoiler.

Authority	x	Powerlessness, anarchy, insubordination.
Autocratic	x	Democratic, responsible, constitutional.
Automatic	x	Unusual, voluntary, optional.
Autonomy	x	Hegemony, captivity, dependence.
Auxiliary	x	Main, major, chief.
Available	x	Unavailable, useless, inoperative.
Avaricious	x	Generous, liberal, bountiful.
Avenge	x	Forgive, pardon, condone.
Aver	x	Refute, deny, contradict.
Average	x	Extreme, perfect, extraordinary.
Aversion	x	Liking, sympathy, affection.
Avidity	x	Apathy, indifference, aversion.
Avoid	x	Seek, approach, affect.
Avouch	x	Deny, contradict, gainsay.
Avow	x	Deny, disavow, ignore.
Awake	x	Asleep, absent, unaware.
Awaken	x	Suppress, allay, restrain.

Award	x	Refuse, withhold, retain.
Aware	x	Unaware, unconscious, ignorant.
Away	x	Near, here, present.
Awe	x	Contempt, reassure, insolence.
Awful	x	Gracious, pleasant, dignified.
Awkward	x	Elegant, relaxed, comfortable, at ease.
Awry	x	Straight, direct, right.
Axim	x	Nonsense, absurdity, contradiction.

B

Babble	x	Silence, quiet, sense.
Babel	x	Calm, order, harmony.
Back	x	Hinder, disappoint, push.
Back	x	Front, preceding, future.
Backbite	x	Cherish, complement, praise.
Backbiter	x	Advocate, upholder, defender.
Backbone	x	Weakness, spinelessness, cowardice.
Backslider	x	Adherent, loyalist, faithful.
Backward	x	Forward, aggressive, head.
Bad	x	Good, right, pleasant.
Baffle	x	Encourage, comfort, aid.
Baked	x	Unbaked, raw, wet.
Balance	x	Imbalance, upset, inequality.

Bald	x	Adorned, hairy, decorated.
Baleful	x	Good, beneficial, favorable.
Balk	x	Aid, accept, meet.
Ballistic	x	Antiballistic, delighted, pleased.
Ban	x	Allow, approve, sanction.
Baneful	x	Benevolent, harmless, innocent.
Banish	x	Repatriate, welcome, accept.
Bankrupt	x	Solvent, rich, filled.
Banquet	x	Fast, starvation, abstinence.
Banter	x	Flattery, praise, work.
Bar	x	Admit, aberration, failure
Barbarian	x	Civilized, cultured, educated.
Barbarous	x	Compassionate, humane, cultured.
Bare	x	Covered, clothed, full.
Bargain	x	Break, disagreement, loss.
Barren	x	Fertile, productive, fruitful.
Barrier	x	Thoroughfare, open, assistance.
Base	x	Noble, honourable, valued.

Bashful	x	Daring, forward, aggressive.
Basis	x	Apex, top, superstructure.
Bathe	x	Dry, ignore, dirty.
Battle	x	Accord, ceasefire, truce.
Beach	x	Ocean, sea, deep.
Beacon	x	Shadow, dark, ignite.
Beam	x	Die out, grow dark, go out.
Bear	x	Drop, avoid, refuse.
Bearable	x	Unbearable, intolerable, inadequate.
Bearded	x	Beardless, shaved, avoid.
Bearing	x	Independence, irrelevancy, absurdity.
Beastly	x	Humane, chivalrous, inoffensive.
Beat	x	Energetic, lively, fresh.
Beat	x	Caress, soothe, pat.
Beatable	x	Unbeatable, unsusceptible, unwearied.
Beatific	x	Sorrowful, demonic, dark.
Beatitude	x	Suffering, trouble, agitation.
Beautiful	x	Ugly, awkward, dull.

Beauty	x	Ugliness, inelegance, crudeness.
Beckon	x	Deter, ignore, repulse.
Become	x	Remain, stagnate, disagree.
Becoming	x	Unbecoming, indecent, derogatory.
Befall	x	Impend, stay, stop.
Befitting	x	Unfitting, inappropriate, imprecise.
Befog	x	Clarify, expose, brighten.
Before	x	After, behind, later.
Beforehand	x	Afterwards, belatedly, later.
Beg	x	Answer, give, replay.
Beget	x	Kill, limit, restrict.
Beggar	x	Capitalist, giver, benefactor.
Beggarly	x	Affluent, wealthy, prosperous.
Beggary	x	Wealth, affluence, abundance.
Begin	x	Stop, cease, conclude.
Beginner	x	Expert, professional, master.
Beginning	x	End, conclusion, termination.
Beguile	x	Disenchant, refuse, offer.

Behavior	x	Misbehavior, repose, cessation.
Behest	x	Answer, replay, liberty.
Behind	x	Ahead, before, in front of.
Behold	x	Ignore, miss, disregard.
Being	x	Abstract, inanimate, nonentity.
Beleaguer	x	Aid, relieve, soothe.
Belief	x	Disbelief, distrust, ignorance.
Believable	x	Unbelievable, incredible, implausible.
Belittle	x	Admire, approve, acclaim.
Belligerent	x	Peaceful, friendly, agreeable.
Belonging	x	Dislike, opposition, antipathy.
Below	x	Above, more, over.
Bend	x	Unbend, straighten, direct.
Beneath	x	Above, higher, over.
Benediction	x	Malediction, curse, condemnation.
Benefactor	x	Opponent, oppressor, antagonist.
Beneficence	x	Malevolence, miserliness, niggardliness.
Beneficial	x	Harmful, injurious, damaging.

Benefit	x	Loss, blockage, damage.
Benevolence	x	Cruelty, meanness, hatred.
Benign	x	Cruel, brutal, unkind.
Bequeath	x	Take, keep, receive.
Bereavement	x	Comfort, consolation, restitution.
Bereft	x	Full, endowed, happy.
Beseech	x	Grant, command, offer.
Beset	x	Clarify, explain, surrender.
Best	x	Worst, inferior, poor.
Bestow	x	Withhold, eject, evict.
Bestow	x	Withhold, receive, take.
Bet	x	Certainty, calculate, dispose.
Betimes	x	Inopportune, late, unseasonable.
Betoken	x	Deny, mask, hide.
Betray	x	Protect, preserve, support.
Betrothal	x	Break, separation, divorce.
Better	x	Worse, inferior, weaken.
Between	x	Outside, beyond, without.

Bewail	x	Rejoice, praise, exult.
Beware	x	Disregard, neglect, ignore.
Bewilder	x	Enlighten, satisfy, comfort.
Bewilderment	x	Expectation, calmness, discernment.
Bewitch	x	Bore, disenchant, disgust.
Beyond	x	Beside, near, below.
Bias	x	Unbiased, fairness, justice.
Bicker	x	Agree, concur, concede.
Bid	x	Forbid, comply, obey.
Bidding	x	Answer, request, rebuff.
Bide	x	Cease, depart, complete.
Big	x	Small, little, humble.
Bigot	x	Moderate, liberal, tolerate.
Bigoted	x	Fair, unprejudiced, broad-minded.
Bilateral	x	Unilateral, one-sided, multilateral.
Bind	x	Loosen, liberate, set free.
Birth	x	Death, extinction, end.
Bit	x	Whole, entirety, lot.

Biting	x	Pleasant, kind, mild.
Bitter	x	Sweet, bland, content.
Blacken	x	Bleach, lighten, complement.
Blackguard	x	Gentleman, hero, cavalier.
Blame	x	Praise, approve, acquit.
Blameless	x	Blamable, culpable, implicated.
Blanch	x	Darken, stain, dye.
Bland	x	Spicy, harsh, rough.
Blandishment	x	Criticism, bluntness, scolding.
Blank	x	Full, aware, dirty.
Blasphemy	x	Respect, reverence, godliness.
Blast	x	Restore, calm, stillness.
Blaze	x	Dimness, blackness, darkness.
Blazon	x	Conceal, deny, cover.
Bleach	x	Blacken, darken, stain.
Bleak	x	Cheerful, bright, warm.
Blemish	x	Purity, blank, clarity.
Blend	x	Severe, division, natural element.

Bless	x	Curse, condemn, castigate.
Blessing	x	Curse, blight, criticism.
Blight	x	Blessing, prosperity, goodness.
Blind	x	Seeing, aware, open.
Blink	x	Attend, notice, be aware.
Bliss	x	Grief, misery, depression.
Blithe	x	Dejected, depressed, worried.
Block	x	Free, clear, whole.
Blockhead	x	Genius, brain, sage.
Bloodless	x	Bloody, blushing, caring.
Bloom	x	Fade, decay, wither.
Blooming	x	Fading, waning, declining.
Blot	x	Cleanse, clear, perpetuate.
Blow	x	Caress, comfort, calm.
Bluff	x	Courteous, polite, refined.
Blunder	x	Correctness, truthfulness, success.
Blunt	x	Sharp, pointed, polished.
Blur	x	Clarity, bright, un cloud.

Blurred	x	Clear, brighten, distinct.
Blush	x	Paleness, pallor, whiteness.
Boast	x	Humility, deprecation, modesty.
Bodily	x	Spiritually, partially, mentally.
Body	x	Mind, inanimate, abstract.
Bogus	x	Real, genuine, authentic
Boil	x	Freeze, cool, calm.
Boisterous	x	Quiet, moderate, peaceful.
Bold	x	Timid, afraid, shy.
Bolster	x	Decrease, block, neglect.
Bombast	x	Modesty, humility, temperance.
Bond	x	Free, parole, unchain.
Bondage	x	Liberty, freedom, independence.
Bondsman	x	Freeman, gentleman, master.
Bonny	x	Ugly, dull, deformed.
Bonus	x	Fine, punishment, loss.
Booby	x	Sage, solon, oracle.
Bookish	x	Ignorant, stupid, illiterate.

Boom	x	Slump, collapse, failure.
Boon	x	Bane, drawback, misfortune.
Boor	x	Gentleman, charmer, courtier.
Boorish	x	Delicate, polite, polished.
Boost	x	Lower, constraint, decline.
Bootless	x	Fruitful, profitable, effective.
Booty	x	Restitution, fine, forfeiture.
Border	x	Inside, mainland, inside.
Bore	x	Charm, delight, please.
Borrow	x	Lend, give, forfeit.
Borrower	x	Lender, abandon, forsake.
Bosom	x	Exteriority, surface, outside.
Boss	x	Worker, poor, unimportant.
Both	x	Neither, each, none.
Bother	x	Calm, pleasure, advantage.
Bottom	x	Top, height, summit.
Bought	x	Sold, pawned, handcraft.
Bound	x	Unbounded, open, unrestricted.

Boundary	x	Interior, inside, start.
Boundless	x	Bounded, restricted, limited.
Bountiful	x	Meager, scarce, selfish.
Bounty	x	Punishment, penalty, stinginess.
Bow	x	Resist, line, straighten.
Boycott	x	Accept, allow, approve.
Boyhood	x	Manhood, adulthood, manly.
Boyish	x	Manly, adult, mature.
Brag	x	Conceal, whine, deprecate.
Braid	x	Unbind, dishevel, unwind.
Branch	x	Trunk, distributary, effluent.
Branch	x	Trunk, whole, company.
Brand	x	Honour, decorate, distinguish.
Brandish	x	Abandon, cover, save.
Bravado	x	Cowardice, fearfulness, modesty.
Brave	x	Cowardly, afraid, shy.
Bravery	x	Cowardice, spinelessness, fear.
Brawny	x	Skinny, slim, fragile.

Breach	x	Agreement, integrity, upholding.
Break	x	Join, fasten, closure.
Breakable	x	Unbreakable, firm, durable.
Breathless	x	Breathy, calm, composed.
Breed	x	Kill, destroy, halt.
Breeding	x	Rudeness, Ill manners, discourtesy.
Brevity	x	Longevity, lengthiness, permanence.
Brew	x	Disperse, break, chill.
Bridle	x	Encouragement, relax, liberation.
Brief	x	Elaborate, expansive, huge.
Bright	x	Gloomy, dull, cloudy.
Brilliant	x	Dull, stupid, obscure.
Bring	x	Send, avoid, transport.
Brisk	x	Slow, lifeless, idle.
Bristling	x	Smooth, soothed, happy.
Brittle	x	Unbreakable, tough, supple.
Broach	x	Dissuade, deny, withdraw.
Broad	x	Narrow, restricted, limited.

Broken	x	Unbroken, perfect, uniform.
Brook	x	Resist, resent, reject.
Brotherhood	x	Sisterhood, divorce, separation.
Brotherly	x	Hostile, unfriendly, unsociable.
Browbeat	x	Aid, rally, support.
Bruise	x	Heal, soothe, alleviate.
Brunt	x	Relaxation, peace, ease.
Brusque	x	Courteous, polite, tactful.
Brutal	x	Kind, gentle, humane.
Buffoon	x	Sage, genius, philosopher.
Build	x	Demolish, raze, destroy.
Building	x	Ruin, demolition, dismantlement.
Bulge	x	Shrink, depression, lack.
Bulk	x	Portion, insignificance, tininess.
Bulwark	x	Harm, injury, hurt.
Bungler	x	Genius, expert, success.
Buoy	x	Swamp, depress, betray.
Buoyant	x	Heavy, depressed, down.

Burden	x	Ease, lightness, contentment.
Burial	x	Exhumation, disinterment, reintroduce.
Burlesque	x	Classic, history, fact.
Burn	x	Extinguish, smother, put out.
Burnish	x	Dull, tarnish, cloud,
Burst	x	Closure, juncture, hold.
Bury	x	Resurrect, exhume, reveal.
Business	x	Entertainment, leisure, inactivity.
Bustle	x	Idleness, inactivity, order.
Busy	x	Free, lazy, unoccupied.
Buxom	x	Flat, lean, petite.
Buy	x	Sell, hawk, vend.
Buyer	x	Seller, owner, marketer.
Bystander	x	Participant, partaker, member

C

Cabal x Dissolution, disunion, legislate.

Cabalistic x Common, known, outward.

Cabin x Mansion, office, palace.

Cacophony x Euphony, harmoniousness, harmony.

Cad x Gentleman, helper, assistance.

Caducity x Adolescence, childhood, youth.

Cage x Liberate, free, release.

Caitiff x Gentleman, hero, philanthropist.

Cajole x Scold, repel, disenchant.

Calamitous x Fortunate, favorable, advantageous.

Calamity x Fortune, blessing, boon.

Calculate x Miscalculate, guess, risk.

Calculating x Uncalculating, rash, careless.

Calculation	x	Foolishness, ignorance, stupidity.
Caliber	x	Inability, incompetence, inadequacy.
Call	x	Conceal, listen, refrain.
Callous	x	Caring, compassionate, feeling.
Callow	x	Experienced, mature, sophisticated.
Calm	x	Agitate, excited, violent.
Calumniate	x	Complement, acclaim, commend.
Calumny	x	Calmness, happiness, kindness.
Came	x	Went, depart, retreat.
Camp	x	Decamp, eject, evict.
Can	x	Cannot, employ, hire.
Cancel	x	Allow, approve, uphold.
Candid	x	Deceitful, cunning, insincere.
Canvass	x	Agree, ignore, neglect.
Capability	x	Inability, incapability, impotence.
Capacity	x	Impotence, inability, incompetence
Capital	x	Minor, nonessential, secondary, unimportant.
Capitulate	x	Conquer, defend, fight.

Caprice	x	Steadfast, constancy, dependability.
Capricious	x	Constant, dependable, steady.
Captious	x	Commendatory, complimentary, praising.
Captivate	x	Disenchant, disillusion, disgust.
Captivity	x	Freedom, liberty, independence.
Capture	x	Release, liberate, acquit.
Care	x	Neglect, carelessness, negligence.
Career	x	Amusement, avocation, recreation.
Careful	x	Careless, thoughtless, unconcerned.
Caress	x	Beat, ignore, annoy.
Caricature	x	Depreciate, minimize, understate.
Caring	x	Uncaring, ignore, negligent.
Carnage	x	Peace, truce, deliverance.
Carnal	x	Spiritual, pure, intellectual.
Carnival	x	Depressed, gloomy, undecorated
Carnivorous	x	Herbivorous, vegetarian, apivorous.
Carol	x	Clash, lament, groan.
Carousal	x	Saving, fast, abstinence.

Carp	x	Approve, applaud, concede.
Carriage	x	Miscarriage, misconduct, conveyance.
Carry	x	Drop, miscarry, lose.
Carved	x	Un carved, demolish, destroyed.
Case	x	Fantasy, eventuality, relief.
Cash	x	Debt, bills, dollar
Cast	x	Catch, keeping, retention
Castigate	x	Compliment, laud, praise
Casual	x	Deliberate, planned, premeditated.
Casuistry	x	Actuality, certainty, truth.
Catalogue	x	Disorganize, delete, non-registration.
Catastrophe	x	Benefit, blessing, favor,
Catch	x	Free, lose, release.
Categorical	x	Conditional, equivocal, implied.
Category	x	Whole, company, being.
Causality	x	Advantage, blessing, fortune.
Causality	x	Consequence, destiny, result.
Cause	x	Effect, aftermath, consequence.

Caution	x	Careless, disregard, neglect.
Cavalier	x	Courteous, humble, polite.
Cavil	x	Accept, approve, concede.
Cavity	x	Obstruction, filling, bulge.
Cease	x	Start, commence, continue.
Celebrate	x	Blame, dishonor, reproach.
Celebration	x	Denunciation, condolence, non-observance.
Celebrity	x	Obscurity, commoner, anonymity.
Celerity	x	Delay, slowness, sluggishness.
Celestial	x	Earthly, worldly, mortal.
Censure	x	Praise, compliment, permit.
Center	x	Exterior, rim, boundary.
Central	x	Remote, inaccessible, inconvenient.
Central	x	Additional, minor, insignificant.
Centralize	x	Decentralize, disperse, distribute.
Centrifugal	x	Centripetal, afferent, centralizing.
Ceremonial	x	Unceremonial, informal, casual.
Ceremonious	x	Unceremonious, informal, simple.

Certain	x	Uncertain, dubious, doubtful.
Certainty	x	Uncertainty, ambiguity, hesitation.
Certify	x	Contradict, decertify, disprove.
Cessation	x	Incessancy, continuity, continuance.
Chafe	x	Conciliate, appease, assist.
Chaff	x	Sense, reason, substance.
Chagrin	x	Delight, comfort, happiness.
Challenge	x	Acceptance, agree, peace.
Champion	x	Traitor, coward, worst.
Chance	x	Designed, foreseeable, certainty.
Change	x	Constancy, uniformity, stagnation.
Change	x	Stay, hold, retain.
Changeable	x	Unchangeable, constant, steady.
Changeless	x	Variable, fluctuating, changeable.
Chaos	x	Order, method, pattern.
Character	x	Anonymousness, disrepute, vagueness.
Characteristic	x	Uncharacteristic, common, usual.
Charge	x	Discharge, acquit, compliment.

Charitable	x	Uncharitable, unkind, harsh, inhuman.
Charity	x	Hindrance, harshness, malevolence.
Charlatan	x	Honesty, dupe, gull.
Charm	x	Ugliness, repulsion, disenchantment.
Chary	x	Careless, incautious, hasty.
Chase	x	Escape, retreat, Flee.
Chaste	x	Corrupt, unchaste, impure.
Chasten	x	Aid, approve, exonerate.
Chattel	x	Freehold, enslaver, master.
Cheap	x	Costly, expensive, precious.
Cheat	x	Truth, reality, sincerity.
Check	x	Allow, permit, liberate.
Checked	x	Unchecked, freedom, continuance.
Cheer	x	Gloom, sorrow, unhappiness.
Cheerful	x	Gloomy, dull, pessimistic.
Cherish	x	Abhor, condemn, dislike.
Chief	x	Subordinate, minor, inferior.
Chieftain	x	Vassal, minion, follower.

Childish	x	Manly, wise, mature.
Chill	x	Warm, bright, cheerful.
Chimerical	x	Realistic, actual, substantial.
Chivalrous	x	Fearful, frightened, humble.
Choice	x	Necessity, compulsion, refusal.
Choice	x	Compulsion, ordinary, inferior.
Choose	x	Abstain, reject, refuse.
Chronicle	x	Legend, romance, tradition.
Cipher	x	Infinity somebody, notability.
Circular	x	Linear, non-cyclic, direct, straight.
Circulate	x	Conceal, suppress, collect.
Circumference	x	Center, interior, inside.
Circumlocution	x	Brevity, compression, directness.
Circumscribe	x	Exceed, expand, amplify.
Circumspect	x	Careless, incautious, heedless.
Circumstance	x	Plan, intend, deed.
Cite	x	Disregard, ignore, conceal.
Citizen	x	Noncitizen, foreigner, alien.

Civilization	x	Barbarism, savagery, retrogression.
Claim	x	Disclaim, challenge, disavowal.
Clamor	x	Quiet, silence, calm.
Clandestine	x	Open, overt, sincere.
Clarity	x	Confusion, un clarity, obscureness.
Class	x	Unstylish, gracelessness, old fashioned.
Classification	x	Disarrange, derange, disorder.
Clause	x	Whole, document, writing.
Clean	x	Unclean, dirty, foul.
Cleanse	x	Pollute, corrupt, adulterate.
Clear	x	Vague, ambiguous, cloudy.
Clever	x	Foolish, ignorant, stupid.
Climax	x	Anticlimax, base, bottom.
Climb	x	Climb down, descent, drop, fall.
Cling	x	Unsticking, unfasten, loose.
Close	x	Distant, far, beyond.
Close	x	Open, spacious, public.
Closure	x	Opening, start, extension.

Cloudy	x	Cloudless, bright, clear.
Clownish	x	Polite, gentle, polished
Clumsy	x	Adroit, expert, coordinated.
Coalesce	x	Split, divide, separate.
Coalition	x	Detachment, disunion, disruption.
Coarse	x	Elegant, fine, dusty
Coax	x	Bug, repel, impel, harass.
Coerce	x	Allow, encourage, help.
Coexistent	x	Unassociated, asynchronous, unrelated.
Cogent	x	Ineffective, feeble, inconclusive.
Cogitate	x	Disregard, overlook, ignore.
Cognizance	x	Disregard, neglect, unawareness.
Coherent	x	Incoherent, illogical, illegitimate.
Coincidence	x	Asynchrony, nonconformity, difference.
Cold	x	Hot, burning, passionate.
Collateral	x	Lineal, direct, oblique.
Colleague	x	Opponent, enemy, competitor.

Collect	x	Disperse, scatter, distribute.
Collision	x	Avoidance, harmony, compliment.
Colloquy	x	Quiet, silence, taciturnity.
Collusion	x	Honesty, frustration, exposure.
Color	x	Paleness, white, transparency.
Combat	x	Truce, concord, harmony.
Combination	x	Division, separation, dissolution.
Come	x	Go, depart, exit.
Comfort	x	Discomfort, unrest, agony.
Comfortable	x	Uncomfortable, miserable, distressed.
Comic	x	Tragic, uncomic, serious.
Command	x	Appeal, petition, plea.
Commemorate	x	Disregard, forget, ignore.
Commence	x	Finish, conclude, terminate.
Commend	x	Hold, blame, retain.
Comment	x	Heedlessness, confuse, ignorance.
Commerce	x	Unemployment, inactivity, boycott.
Commit	x	Abstain, give up, disregard.

Commodious	x	Confined, narrow, cramped.
Commodity	x	Nonentity, drug, refuse.
Common	x	Uncommon, exceptional, scarce.
Commotion	x	Peace, quiet, tranquility.
Communicate	x	Conceal, hide, suppress.
Communion	x	Alienation, disaffection, antagonism.
Community	x	Difference, dissimilarity, individualist.
Commute	x	Increase, enlarge, keep.
Compact	x	Loose, empty, uncondensed.
Companion	x	Rival, antagonist, adversary.
Companionable	x	Antagonistic, hostile, unfriendly.
Company	x	Forlornness, loneliness, privacy.
Compare	x	Contrast, discern, differentiate.
Compass	x	Freedom, infinity, interior.
Compassion	x	Cruelty, animosity, antipathy.
Compatible	x	Hostile, disagreeable, conflicting.
Compel	x	Allow, permit, dissuade.
Compensation	x	Debt, hurt, nonpayment.

Compete	x	Agree, give up, share.
Competence	x	Incompetence, inability, ineptness.
Competition	x	Alliance, accord, harmony.
Complacent	x	Concerned, interested, unsure.
Complain	x	Accept, approve, rejoice.
Complement	x	Base, decrease, deficiency.
Complete	x	Incomplete, imperfect, partial.
Complex	x	Noncomplex, simple, homogeneous.
Compliance	x	Resistance, defiance, refusal.
Complicated	x	Simple, easy, plain.
Compliment	x	Blame, affront, contempt.
Complimentary	x	Depreciative, paid, unmannerly.
Component	x	Whole, compound, aggregate.
Comport	x	Differ, disagree, contradict.
Compose	x	Discompose, break, agitate.
Composition	x	Disproportion, segregation, imbalance.
Composure	x	Agitation, discomposure, perturbation.

Compound	x	Non- compound, division, separation.
Comprehend	x	Misapprehend, misunderstand, exclude.
Comprehension	x	Incomprehension, ignorance, inability.
Comprehensive	x	Circumscribed, empty, narrow.
Compress	x	Amplify, expand, decompress.
Comprise	x	Abandon, exclude, reject.
Compromise	x	Denial, disagreement, refusal.
Compulsion	x	Agreement, free will, independence.
Compulsory	x	Voluntary, option, elective.
Compunction	x	Assurance, disdain, aplomb.
Compute	x	Estimate, surmise, guess.
Comrade	x	Rival, adversary, enemy.
Concatenation	x	Interruption, severing, disconnection.
Concave	x	Convex, distended, bulging.
Conceal	x	Reveal, expose, exhibit.
Concede	x	Defend, disallow, deny.
Conceit	x	Reality, humility, actuality.

Conceited	x	Humble, diffident, egoless.
Conceive	x	Misconceive, neglect, execute.
Concentrate	x	Dilute, scatter, unsettle.
Concept	x	Reality, concrete, actuality.
Concern	x	Unconcern, indifference, content.
Concert	x	Discord, opposition, disagreement.
Concession	x	Refusal, denial, disavowal.
Conciliate	x	Incite, irritate, estrange.
Concise	x	Elaborate, lengthy, circuitous.
Conclave	x	Throng, mob, populace.
Conclude	x	Begin, commence, initiate.
Conclusion	x	Commencement, beginning, initiation.
Conclusive	x	Inconclusive, ambiguous, debatable.
Concoct	x	Demolish, destroy, clone.
Concomitant	x	Unassociated, unconnected, accidental.
Concord	x	Discord, conflict, agitation.
Concourse	x	Conclave, desert, solitude.

Concrete	x	Loose, abstract, general.
Concrete	x	Alleged, assumed, supposed.
Concussion	x	Inter-divergence, escape, tangency.
Condemn	x	Bless, approve, endorse.
Condense	x	Expand, enlarge, outstretch.
Condescend	x	Contradict, dispute, rise.
Condign	x	Undeserved, undue, inadequate.
Condition	x	Disorder, concession, dependence.
Conditionally	x	Unconditionally, absolutely, positively.
Condole	x	Annoy, disregard, trouble.
Condone	x	Heed, object, satisfy.
Conduce	x	Block, impede, counteract.
Conduct	x	Misconduct, mismanage, disregard.
Confederacy	x	Secession, disruption, disunion.
Conference	x	Silence, monologue, dispersion.
Confess	x	Deny, conceal, disavow, hide, dissemble.
Confession	x	Denial, refusal, repudiation
Confide	x	Detain, conceal, doubt.

Confident	x	Doubtful, diffident, afraid
Confidential	x	Public, revealed, open.
Configuration	x	Disarrangement, shapelessness, distortion.
Confine	x	Free, widen, liberate.
Confirm	x	Decline, deny, cancel.
Confiscate	x	Release, restore, refund.
Conflagration	x	Peace, truce, dis-armament.
Conflict	x	Harmony, reconciliation, pacification.
Conform	x	Disagree, differ, prevent.
Confound	x	Calm, clear, restore.
Confront	x	Avoid, shun, surrender.
Confuse	x	Clarify, simplify, calm.
Congeal	x	Melt, soften, deliquesce.
Congenial	x	Disagreeable, abominable, unsociable.
Congenital	x	Unnatural, contracted, acquired.
Congeries	x	Dissipation, dispersion, clearance.
Congratulate	x	Blame, condemn, belittle.
Congregate	x	Disperse, separate, scatter.

Congregation	x	Dispersion, dismissal, division.
Congress	x	Division, lawlessness, intrigue.
Congruous	x	Discordant, heterogeneous, unsuitable.
Conjecture	x	Calculation, inference, certainty.
Conjuncture	x	Provision, preparation, cessation.
Connect	x	Disconnect, disjoin, detach.
Connection	x	Disconnection, independence, rift.
Conquer	x	Relinquish, surrender, retreat.
Conquerable	x	Unconquerable, indomitable, unsusceptible.
Conquest	x	Defeat, surrender, submission.
Conscience	x	Irresponsibility, laxity, immorality.
Conscientious	x	Careless, uncritical, indifferent.
Conscious	x	Unconscious, unaware, ignorant.
Conscription	x	Volunteering, enlistment, enrollment.
Consecrate	x	Deconsecrate, desecrate, defile.
Consecutive	x	Inconsecutive, infrequent, interrupted.
Consensus	x	Discord, conflict, disagreement.

Consent	x	Object, refuse, reject.
Consequence	x	Cause, basis, origin.
Consequential	x	Insignificant, unimportant, paltry.
Conservation	x	Neglect, destruction, abolition.
Conservative	x	Radical, reactionary, changeable.
Consider	x	Discount, disregard, ignore.
Considerable	x	Negligible, diminutive, little.
Considerate	x	Inconsiderate, merciless, uncaring.
Consignee	x	Consignor, donor, giver.
Consistency	x	Inconsistency, erraticism, incongruity.
Consolation	x	Tribulation, disdain, distress.
Console	x	Distress, upset, agitate.
Consolidate	x	Dissolve, segregate, weaken.
Conspicuous	x	Invisible, hidden, indistinct.
Constant	x	Irregular, incidental, temporary.
Consternation	x	Fearlessness, contentment, composure.
Constituent	x	Aggregate, composite, auxiliary.

Constitution	x	Disarrangement, disorganization, destruction.
Construct	x	Demolish, destroy, derange.
Construction	x	Destruction, disfigurement, ruin.
Consult	x	Dictate, neglect, ignore.
Consume	x	Unconsumed, discard, preserve.
Consummate	x	Inept, imperfect, incapable.
Consummation	x	Beginning, inception, introduction.
Consumption	x	Production, development, creation.
Contact	x	Avoidance, division, separation.
Contagion	x	Prevention; purification, disinfection.
Contain	x	Exclude, omit, leave.
Contaminate	x	Decontaminate, Cleanse, purify.
Contemn	x	Cherish, respect, admire.
Contemplate	x	Forget, reject, neglect.
Contemptible	x	Respectable, delightful, admirable.
Contend	x	Concede, allow, surrender.
Content	x	Discontent, displeased, unsatisfied.
Contention	x	Peace, accord, harmony.

Contingent	x	Independent, designed, uncontrolled.
Continual	x	Bounded, discontinuous, broken.
Continually	x	Occasionally, infrequently, rarely.
Continue	x	Discontinue, cease, pause.
Contract	x	Disagreement, misunderstanding, Promise.
Contraction	x	Expansion, cancel, abandon.
Contradict	x	Admit, agree, allow.
Contrary	x	Agreeable, compatible, consistent.
Contrast	x	Resemble, similarity, alikeness.
Contribute	x	Hold, keep, deny.
Contrive	x	Break, destroy, replicate.
Control	x	Freedom, chaos, neglect.
Controllable	x	Uncontrollable, unmanageable, weakness.
Controversy	x	Agreement, concurrence, peace.
Controvert	x	Assert, affirm, co-exist.
Contumely	x	Admiration, approval, respect.
Convene	x	Dismiss, disperse, disband.

Convenient	x	Inconvenient, useless, harmful.
Convention	x	Discord, dissolution, strangeness.
Conventional	x	Unconventional, Unusual, abnormal.
Converge	x	Diverge, disperse, disband.
Conversant	x	Ignorant, unaware, unlearned.
Converse	x	Identical, same, equal.
Conversion	x	Permanence, stagnation, persistence.
Convertible	x	Variant, contrary, incommensurate.
Convex	x	Concave, biconcave, distress.
Convey	x	Receive, retain, take.
Convict	x	Acquit, victim, absolve.
Convicted	x	Acquitted, free, release.
Conviction	x	Doubt, disbelief, incertitude.
Convince	x	Deter, discourage, dissuade.
Convincing	x	Unconvincing, ineffective, inconclusive.
Convivial	x	Inhospitable, antisocial, apathetic.
Convocation	x	Dispersion, disruption, dismissal.
Convolution	x	Straightness, line, unraveling

Convoy	x	Abandon, betrayal, ditch.
Convulse	x	Calm, compose, soothe.
Cool	x	Hot, responsive, warm.
Cooperate	x	Oppose, obstruct, hinder.
Cooperation	x	Non-cooperation, disassociation, disunion.
Coordinate	x	Subordinate, disparate, inferior.
Copy	x	Original, prototype, exemplar.
Cordial	x	Cool, hostile, unfriendly.
Corner	x	Centre, middle, prominence.
Corollary	x	Antecedent, causation, beginning.
Corporal	x	Spiritual, mental, immaterial.
Corps	x	Connection, whole, individual.
Corpse	x	Soul, personality, mentality.
Corpulent	x	Lean, thin, slender.
Correct	x	Incorrect, wrong, inaccurate.
Corrective	x	Damaging, confirmative, harmful.
Correlation	x	Difference, disassociation, disconnection.

Correspond	x	Differ, disagree, clash.
Correspondence	x	Difference, dissimilarity, discord.
Corrigible	x	Incorrigible, unredeemable, irreparable.
Corroborate	x	Contradict, disapprove, invalidate.
Corrode	x	Freshen, recreate, build.
Corrupt	x	Uncorrupt, honest, ethical.
Costume	x	Disguise, incognito, nudity.
Council	x	Individual, one, conspiracy.
Count	x	Guess, estimate, part.
Countable	x	Countless, incalculable, inestimable.
Countenance	x	Alarm, anxiety, agitation.
Counter	x	Support, harmonious, agreeing.
Counteract	x	Aid, assist, allow.
Counterfeit	x	Genuine, actual, authentic.
Countermand	x	Approve, permit, enforce.
Counterpart	x	Original, opposite, antithesis.
Countryman	x	Alien, cosmopolitan, immigrant.
Couple	x	Separate, detach, isolate.

Courage	x	Cowardice, fear, dread.
Course	x	Deviation, disorder, hindrance.
Court	x	Avoid, shun, repudiate.
Courteous	x	Discourteous, rude, impolite.
Courtesy	x	Disdain, disregard, disrespect.
Courtly	x	Rustic, undignified, impolite.
Covenant	x	Disagreement, misunderstanding, denial.
Cover	x	Uncover, expose, exhibit.
Covert	x	Open, exposed, public.
Covet	x	Dislike, hate, abjure.
Covetous	x	Generous, benevolent, charitable.
Coward	x	Brave, champion, valiant.
Cowardice	x	Bravery, courage, boldness.
Coy	x	Impudent, immodest, aggressive.
Crack	x	Inept, inferior, unfit.
Craft	x	Inaptitude, artlessness, clumsiness.
Crafty	x	Candid, innocent, artless.
Cramp	x	Comfort, ease, relieve.

Crash	x	Victory, accomplishment, failure.
Crave	x	Apathy, spurn, dislike.
Crazy	x	Sane, balanced, reasonable.
Create	x	Destroy, demolish, annihilate.
Creature	x	Inanimate, abstract, plant.
Credence	x	Denial, distrust, doubt.
Credible	x	Incredible, improbable, unreliable.
Credit	x	Discredit, distrust, debit.
Creditor	x	Debtor, donor, giver.
Credulity	x	Skepticism, disbelief, incredulity.
Creed	x	Agnosticism, atheism, disbelief.
Crestfallen	x	Cheerful, elated, blissful.
Crew	x	Individual, whole, one.
Crime	x	Non-crime, goodness, virtue.
Criminal	x	Lawful, virtuous, legitimate
Criminate	x	Acquit, absolve, extricate.
Cripple	x	Aid, assist, strengthen.
Criterion	x	Conjecture, aberration, deviation.

Critic	x	Reviewer, amateur, performer.
Critical	x	Uncritical, safe, trivial.
Criticism	x	Praise, approval, heedlessness.
Criticize	x	Approve, commend, praise.
Crooked	x	Straight, linear, unbent.
Cross	x	Amiable, genial, purebred.
Crowd	x	Loner, individualist, single.
Crown	x	Base, bottom, shame.
Crucial	x	Inessential, insignificant, unimportant.
Crude	x	Refined, clean, decent.
Cruel	x	Kind, compassionate, gentle.
Cry	x	Laugh, murmur, whisper.
Culmination	x	Anticlimax, nadir, decline.
Culpable	x	Inculpable, blameless, immune.
Culprit	x	Accuser, saint, upright man.
Cultivate	x	Debase, abandon, destroy.
Cultured	x	Uncultured, ignorant, barbaric.
Cunning	x	Frank, clever, sincerity.

Cupidity	x	Contentment, apathy, generosity.
Curable	x	Incurable, unhardened, un tempered.
Curb	x	Encourage, freedom, release.
Cure	x	Injury, hurt, disease.
Curiosity	x	Indifference, disinterest, incuriosity.
Curious	x	Incurious, unconcerned, indifferent.
Current	x	Antiquated, old-fashioned, uncommon.
Curse	x	Blessing, benediction, boon.
Cursory	x	Detailed, deliberate, elaborate.
Custody	x	Neglect, desertion; liberation.
Custom	x	Deviation, regulation, difference.
Customer	x	Seller, vendor, broker.
Cutting	x	Calm, mild, soothing.
Cynical	x	Considerate, believing, optimistic.

D

Dabbler	x	Professional, expert, specialist.
Daft	x	Sensible, rational, clear.
Dainty	x	Coarse, crude, unrefined.
Damage	x	Construction, benefit, advantage.
Damn	x	Support, bless, pardon.
Danger	x	Safety, guard, security.
Daring	x	Afraid, cautious, coward.
Dark	x	Bright, light, luminous.
Darling	x	Enemy, estranged, hate.
Dash	x	Slowness, drab, lethargy.
Dastard	x	Hero, champion, valiant
Data	x	Conjectures, assumptions, inferences.
Daub	x	Clean, purify, cleanse.

Daunt	x	Encourage, assist, comfort.
Dauntless	x	Afraid, cowardly, nervous.
Dawn	x	Dusk, end, close.
Dazzle	x	Bore, dark, dullness.
Dead	x	Alive, fresh, rejuvenated.
Deadly	x	Vital, harmless, life-giving.
Deaf	x	Attentive, aware, conscious.
Deal	x	Denial, stop, dissension.
Dear	x	Cheap, hateful, valueless.
Dearth	x	Plenty, abundance, luxury.
Death	x	Birth, life, creation.
Debar	x	Admit, allow, include.
Debase	x	Dignify, honour, elevate.
Debatable	x	Irrefutable, definite, settled.
Debate	x	Accord, agreement, compliance.
Debauch	x	Dignify, loyalty, exalt.
Debility	x	Vigor, strength. vitality.
Debit	x	Credit, asset, advantage.

Debt	x	Excess, assets, profit.
Debtor	x	Creditor, lender, mortgagee.
Decay	x	Construction, growth, improvement.
Deceit	x	Honesty, integrity, sincerity.
Deceive	x	Undeceive, protect, support.
Decent	x	Indecent, improper, unreliable.
Deception	x	Honesty, sincerity, frankness.
Decide	x	Waver, abort, call off.
Decipher	x	Conceal, encode, jumble up.
Decision	x	Indecision, refusal, uncertainty.
Decisive	x	Inconclusive, indefinite, irresolute.
Deck	x	Disfigure, spoil, unclothe.
Declaim	x	Compliment, praise, be quiet.
Declaration	x	Denial, disclaimer, disavowal.
Declare	x	Conceal, suppress, contradict.
Decline	x	Increase, rise, success.
Declivity	x	Ascent, acclivity, up rise.
Decompose	x	Compose, develop, mature.

Decorate	x	Deface, darken, disfigure.
Decorum	x	Indecorum, impropriety, disorder.
Decrease	x	Increase, enlargement, rise.
Decree	x	Appeal, proposal, request.
Decrepit	x	Firm, healthy, strong.
Decry	x	Approve, praise, laud.
Dedicate	x	Ignore, misuse, hold.
Deduce	x	Induce, destroy, disperse.
Deed	x	Idleness, inaction, failure.
Deep	x	Shallow; superficial, narrow.
Deface	x	Decorate, conserve, build.
Defame	x	Praise, glorify, compliment.
Default	x	Accuracy, abundance, compliance.
Defeat	x	Win, accomplishment, triumph.
Defect	x	Adornment, decoration, correction.
Defend	x	Undefend, attack, abandon.
Defense	x	Aggression, assault, surrender.
Defer	x	Advance, expedite, decide.

Deference	x	Animosity, fight, defiance.
Defiant	x	Obedient, acquiescent, amenable.
Deficit	x	Surplus, abundance, plentiful.
Defile	x	Elevate, honour, praise.
Definite	x	Indefinite, ambiguous, implicit.
Definition	x	Question, ambiguity, nonsense.
Deflate	x	Inflate, increase, expand.
Deformity	x	Beauty, benefit, adornment.
Defrayment	x	Debt, loss, penalty.
Defy	x	Comply, aid, respect.
Degeneracy	x	Ascent, honour, development.
Degrade	x	Upgrade, elevate, advance.
Dejected	x	Cheerful, elated, blissful.
Delay	x	Hurry, haste, continuation.
Delegate	x	Substitute, proxy, detain.
Delegate	x	Relegate, recall, supersede.
Deleterious	x	Advantageous, beneficial, helpful.
Deliberate	x	Unintentional, casual, careless.

Delicacy	x	Indelicacy, coarseness, strength.
Delicious	x	Distasteful, bitter, nasty.
Delight	x	Discontent, pain, sorrow.
Delightful	x	Sadness, sorrow, unhappiness.
Delineate	x	Confuse, distort, falsify.
Delinquent	x	Early, inopportune, premature.
Deliver	x	Confine, keep, retain.
Deluge	x	Drought, drip, moisture.
Delusion	x	Fact, actuality, truth.
Demand	x	Offer, surplus, waive.
Demarcation	x	Openness, blurring, confusion.
Demean	x	Admire, dignify, elevate.
Dement	x	Appease, balance, calm.
Demerit	x	Merit, excellence, virtue.
Democratic	x	Undemocratic, nondemocratic, autocratic.
Demolish	x	Build, construct, erect.
Demonstration	x	Concealment, contradiction, denial.
Demoralize	x	Encourage, strengthen, uplift.

Demure	x	Bold, brave, extrovert.
Denial	x	Confirmation, approval, allowance.
Denizen	x	Foreigner, alien, stranger.
Denomination	x	Agnosticism, atheism, disbelief.
Denounce	x	Bless, applaud, exonerate.
Dense	x	Sparse, clear, scattered.
Denunciation	x	Compliment, acclamation, endorsement.
Deny	x	Accept, approve, admit.
Depart	x	Arrive, occupy, stay.
Dependent	x	Independent, strong, free.
Depict	x	Hide, suppress, conceal.
Deplorable	x	Acceptable, bearable, pleasing.
Depose	x	Allow, enthrone, elevate.
Deprecate	x	Approve, commend, sanction.
Depreciate	x	Appreciate, acclaim, build.
Depredation	x	Boon, goodness, amends.
Depression	x	Advantage, development, improvement.
Deprive	x	Invest, compensate, elect.

Deputy	x	Chief, Manager, principal.
Derangement	x	Order, dislocation, sanity.
Derision	x	Admiration, respect, applaud.
Derivation	x	Completion, termination, original.
Derogate	x	Acclaim, compliment, praise.
Descend	x	Ascend, improve, mount.
Descendant	x	Ascendant, predecessor, source.
Describe	x	Distort, ignore, confuse.
Descry	x	Overlook, miss, neglect.
Desecrate	x	Honour, protect, sanctify.
Desert	x	Inhabited, populated, cultivated.
Deserter	x	Adherent, loyalist, disciple.
Deserve	x	Forfeit, fail, spend.
Deserved	x	Undeserved, undue, unfair.
Desideratum	x	Dislike, hate, surplus.
Designate	x	Discharge, dismiss, misrepresent.
Desirable	x	Undesirable, disadvantageous, harmful.
Desire	x	Aversion, hate, repugnance.

Desolate	x	Populated, frequented, bright.
Despair	x	Hope, cheer, comfort.
Desperate	x	Hopeful, elated, optimistic.
Despise	x	Desire, admire, cherish.
Despoil	x	Build, clothe, guard.
Despotic	x	Restricted, limited, representative.
Destination	x	Beginning, source, start.
Destiny	x	Choice, freedom, volition.
Destitute	x	Affluent, prosperous, filled.
Destructive	x	Constructive, protective, creative.
Desuetude	x	Use, custom, operation.
Desultory	x	Organized, methodical, systematic.
Detach	x	Attach, associate, unite.
Detail	x	Entirety, generality, totality.
Detain	x	Promote, discharge, liberate.
Detention	x	Release, discharge, freedom.
Deter	x	Incite, advance, persuade.
Deteriorate	x	Improve, advance, strengthen.

Determine	x	Abstain, hinder, suppress
Detest	x	Desire, admire, love.
Dethrone	x	Crown, enthrone, exalt.
Detract	x	Develop, concentrate, optimize.
Develop	x	Abandon, decline, stunt.
Deviate	x	Common, straiten, stay.
Devious	x	Direct, fair, straightforward.
Devise	x	Destroy, clone, duplicate.
Devoid	x	Full, complete, supplied.
Devolve	x	Ameliorate, improve, meliorate.
Devoted	x	Apathetic, irresponsible, disloyal
Devotion	x	Animosity, disregard, apathy.
Devour	x	Build, create, replace.
Dexterity	x	Ineptitude, ignorance, inability.
Diagnosis	x	Deadlock, draw, halt.
Diagnostic	x	Atypical, uncharacteristic, development.
Dialogue	x	Monologue, soliloquy, silent.
Dictate	x	Follow, obey, accept.

Dictation	x	Consultation, conference, advice.
Dictatorial	x	Democratic, obedient, persuasive.
Die	x	Live, exist, begin.
Diet	x	Starvation, abstinence, indulgence.
Difference	x	Agreement, resemblance, similarity.
Differentiate	x	Misinterpret, amalgamate, associate.
Difficult	x	Easy, trivial, simple.
Diffident	x	Bold, aggressive, confident.
Diffuse	x	Concise, concentrated, brief.
Dignified	x	Undignified, ignoble.
Dignify	x	Degrade, condemn, dishonor.
Dignity	x	Indignity, degradation, subordination.
Digress	x	Stay, proceed, advance.
Dilapidation	x	Inattention, repair, construction.
Dilate	x	Contract, abbreviate, condense.
Dilatory	x	Prompt, diligent, enthusiastic.
Diligence	x	Neglect, carelessness, inactivity.
Dilute	x	Concentrated, enrich, aggravate.

Dim	x	Bright, cheerful, light.
Dimension	x	Insignificance, unimportant, segment.
Diminish	x	Magnify, develop, increase.
Din	x	Calm, order, silence.
Dingy	x	Bright, clean, sterile.
Dip	x	Dry, ascent, increase.
Diplomacy	x	Tactlessness, impoliteness, ignorance.
Diplomatic	x	Untactful, impolite, rude.
Direct	x	Indirect, ambiguous, crooked.
Direction	x	Deviation, misdirection, wrong way.
Directly	x	Indirectly, inexactly, inexactly.
Dirge	x	Paean, encomium, panegyric.
Dirt	x	Cleanness, purity, spotlessness.
Dirty	x	Clean, pure, unstained.
Disability	x	Ability, merit, strength.
Disabuse	x	Limit, delude, beguile.
Disagree	x	Agree, assent, consent.
Disappear	x	Appear, emerge, arrive.

Disappoint	x	Satisfy, fulfill, content.
Disapprove	x	Approve, allow, sanction.
Disaster	x	Blessing, achievement, boon.
Disband	x	Organize, assemble, incorporate.
Disbelief	x	Belief, conviction, certainty
Disburse	x	Acquire, gather, hoard.
Discern	x	Overlook, confuse, miss.
Discernible	x	Ambiguous, obscure, impalpable.
Discernment	x	Stupidity, dullness, density.
Discharge	x	Confine, charge, assignment.
Disciple	x	Detractor, enemy, leader.
Discipline	x	Indiscipline, agitation, disorder.
Disclose	x	Cover, conceal, suppress.
Discomfit	x	Comfort, encourage, aid.
Disconcert	x	Calm, comfort, console.
Disconsolate	x	Cheerful, optimistic, consoled.
Discordance	x	Accordance, agreement, concordance.
Discourage	x	Encourage, assure, animate.

Discourteous	x	Courteous, humble, gracious.
Discover	x	Un discover, hide, ignore.
Discreet	x	Careless, heedless, imprudent.
Discrepancy	x	Accord, similarity, agreement.
Discrimination	x	Equity, fairness, confusion.
Discursive	x	Orderly, coherent, consistent.
Discuss	x	Agree, ignore, neglect.
Disdain	x	Admiration, affection, reverence.
Disease	x	Health, strength, wellness.
Disgrace	x	Honour, esteem, admiration.
Disgust	x	Approval, liking, loving.
Dishonest	x	Honest, truthful, ethical.
Dismal	x	Cheerful, bright, optimistic.
Dismay	x	Assurance, great, marvelous.
Dismember	x	Assemble, construct, erect.
Dismiss	x	Join, keep, recruit.
Disorder	x	Order, method, fitness.
Disown	x	Own, accept, acknowledge.

Disparage	x	Approve, admire, honor.
Disparity	x	Parity, identicalness, agreement.
Dispel	x	Accept, collect, assemble.
Dispensation	x	Denial, gather, disfavour.
Display	x	Concealment, hide, modesty.
Disposition	x	Disinclination, accumulation, confusion.
Disputant	x	Fan, supporter, partner.
Dispute	x	Acceptance, concord, harmony.
Disqualify	x	Qualify, permit, include.
Disregard	x	Regard, concern, attention.
Dissect	x	Combine, integrate, unite.
Dissemble	x	Disclose, reveal, confess.
Dissent	x	Assent, acceptance, concurrence.
Dissipate	x	Assemble, hoard, conserve.
Dissociate	x	Associate, join, affiliate.
Dissolute	x	Pure, uncorrupt, upright.
Dissuade	x	Persuade, encourage, prompt.
Distance	x	Height, proximity, nearness.

Distend	x	Abbreviate, compress, reduce.
Distil	x	Condense, muddy, gush.
Distinct	x	Indistinct, dim, indefinite, obscure.
Distinguish	x	Confuse, mistake, connect.
Distinguished	x	Insignificant, obscure, infamous.
Distortion	x	Beauty, clarity, perfection.
Distract	x	Concentrate, focus, calm.
Distraction	x	Calm, composure, order.
Distress	x	Comfort, consolation, blessing.
Distribute	x	Collect, gather, reserve.
Distrust	x	Trust, credence, faith.
Disturb	x	Calm, assist, compose.
Disturbed	x	Undisturbed, systematic, organised.
Diversify	x	Continue, fix, remain.
Diversion	x	Directness, conformity, adherence.
Diversity	x	Unity, similarity, agreement.
Divest	x	Clothe, give, offer.
Divide	x	Unite, assemble, combine.

Divination	x	Investigation, information, analysis.
Divisible	x	Indivisible, inseparable, combinable.
Divorce	x	Marry, unite, agreement.
Dizzy	x	Steady, unshaken, conscious.
Do	x	Undo, abstain, neglect.
Docile	x	Obstinate, determined, defiant.
Doctrine	x	Ambiguity, disbelief, heterodoxy.
Dogmatic	x	Practical, ambiguous, impartial.
Domestic	x	Wild, foreign, alien.
Dominance	x	Subjection, subordination, weakness.
Domineer	x	Submit, yield, assist.
Dominion	x	Submission, subordination, servitude.
Doom	x	Rise, boon, blessing.
Dormant	x	Active, aware, conscious.
Double	x	Single, singular, unpaired.
Doubt	x	Conviction, certainty, belief.
Doubtful	x	Doubtless, certain, undoubted.
Down	x	Up, elevated, upward.

Downwards	x	Upwards, lifted, raised.
Drag	x	Assist, push, raise.
Drain	x	Fill, strengthen, revive.
Draw	x	Repel, repulse, push.
Dread	x	Pleasant, soothing, familiarity.
Dream	x	Fact, reality, concrete.
Dreary	x	Cheerful, bright, inviting.
Dress	x	Undress, nakedness, nudity.
Drink	x	Pour, exude, disgorge.
Drive	x	Draw, attract, summon.
Droll	x	Boring, grave, tragic.
Droop	x	Prosper, bloom, raise.
Drown	x	Dry, drain, empty.
Dry	x	Wet, damp, moist.
Dubious	x	Sure, decisive, certain.
Due	x	Undue, improper, paid.
Dull	x	Bright, active, exciting.
Dumb	x	Talkative, eloquent, fluent.

Duplicate	x	Original, different, unequal.
Duplicity	x	Candor, frankness, sincerity.
Duration	x	Cessation, closeness, stoppage.
Dusk	x	Dawn, daybreak, ablaze.
Dutiful	x	Undutiful, disrespectful, offensive.
Duty	x	Exemption, freedom, entertainment.
Dwarf	x	Giant, jumbo, monster.
Dwell	x	Move, abscond, escape.
Dwindle	x	Swell, ascent, expand.
Dynamic	x	Static, nonassertive, guarded.

E

Eager	x	Indifferent, casual, apathetic.
Early	x	Late, delayed, expected.
Earn	x	Spend, forfeit, surrender.
Earnest	x	Apathetic, indifferent, dispassionate.
Earthly	x	Heavenly, spiritual, unearthly.
Ease	x	Discomfort, agony, agitation.
East	x	West, westerly, western.
Easy	x	Difficult, complicated, exhausting.
Eat	x	Vomit, abstain, fast.
Ebb	x	Flow, ascend, advance.
Eccentric	x	Normal, common, conventional.
Echo	x	Difference, opposite, reverse.
Eclipse	x	Increase, restoration, advancement.

Economy	x	Diseconomy, wastefulness, extravagance.
Ecstasy	x	Depression, misery, sadness.
Edge	x	Center, bottom, interior.
Edible	x	Inedible, poisonous, harmful.
Edict	x	Request, appeal, proposal.
Edifice	x	Ruin, heap, demolition.
Edit	x	Distort, disarrange, scatter.
Educated	x	Uneducated, neglect, confuse.
Education	x	Ignorance, illiteracy, neglect.
Educe	x	Decrease, repulse, halt.
Efface	x	Restore, conserve, build.
Effect	x	Cause, source, origin.
Effective	x	Ineffective, fruitless, inadequate.
Effectuate	x	Abandon, impede, restrict.
Effeminate	x	Manly, masculine, vigorous.
Effervesce	x	Subside, refrain, digest.
Effete	x	Mighty, powerful, capable.
Efficacious	x	Incapable, insufficient, impotent.

Efficacy	x	Inadequacy, ineffectiveness, inability.
Efficiency	x	Inability, incompetence, ignorance.
Efficient	x	Inactive, delicate, idle.
Effluence	x	Influx, infusion, retention.
Effort	x	Idleness, inactivity, incompetence.
Effrontery	x	Modesty, timidity, bashfulness.
Effulgence	x	Dimness, dullness, darkness.
Effusive	x	Apathetic, reserved, restrained.
Egoism	x	Altruism, selflessness, humility.
Egregious	x	Concealed, imperceptible, mild.
Egress	x	Ingress, entrance, access.
Eject	x	Accept, retain, permit.
Elaborate	x	Short, simple, unrefined.
Elapse	x	Extend, continue, prolong.
Elastic	x	Rigid, inelastic, inflexible.
Elated	x	Dejected, depressed, disappointed.
Elder	x	Younger, junior, inferior.
Elect	x	Reject, abstain, dismiss.

Elegance	x	Inelegance, gracelessness, coarseness.
Elegant	x	Dull, inferior, ugly.
Elegy	x	Encomium, Paean, jubilee, eulogy.
Element	x	Whole, details, total.
Elementary	x	Advanced, compounded, secondary.
Elevate	x	Drop, lower, degrade.
Elevation	x	Degradation, debasement, depression.
Elicit	x	Give, placate, disregard.
Eligible	x	Ineligible, unacceptable, improper.
Elimination	x	Inclusion, retention, addition.
Elision	x	Increase, insertion, inclusion.
Elliptical	x	Pleonastic, redundant, repetitious.
Elongation	x	Abridgment, shortening, abbreviation.
Eloquence	x	Inarticulateness, impotence, inability.
Elucidate	x	Confuse, obscure, befog.
Elucidation	x	Complication, confusion, ambiguity.
Elude	x	Abet, accept, incur.

Elusive	x	Stable, definite, unequivocal.
Emaciation	x	Obesity, fatness, corpulence.
Emanate	x	Conceal, absorb, inhale.
Emancipate	x	Detain, imprison, incapacitate.
Embalm	x	Abandon, neglect, squander.
Embargo	x	Sufferance, assistance, enabling.
Embark	x	Conclude, cease, conclude.
Embarrass	x	Appease, calm, clarify.
Embellish	x	Decrease, lessen, deface.
Embezzle	x	Give, receive, compensate.
Embitter	x	Endear, soothe, comfort.
Emblem	x	Disguise, decoy, incognito.
Embody	x	Disembody, obscure, cover.
Embolden	x	Discourage, depress, daunt.
Embosomed	x	Exposed, open, unconcealed.
Embrace	x	Release, reject, exclude.
Embroider	x	Harm, belittle, understate.
Embroil	x	Emancipate, exclude, untangle.

Embryo	x	Development, completion, maturity.
Emendation	x	Error, defect, inaccuracy.
Emerge	x	Abandon, disappear, decrease.
Emergency	x	Calmness, ease, peace.
Emigration	x	Immigration, settlement, arrival.
Eminence	x	Insignificant, obscurity, unimportant.
Eminent	x	Mediocre, common, unremarkable.
Emission	x	Concealment, suppression, refrain.
Emit	x	Absorb, retain, suck.
Emollient	x	Irritant, astringent, irritating.
Emolument	x	Loss, damage, waste.
Emotion	x	Indifference, insensitiveness, apathy.
Emphasis	x	Deemphasize, indifference, disregard.
Emphatic	x	Non-assertive, mild, unimportant.
Empire	x	Subservience, weakness, independence.
Empirical	x	Non-empirical, hypothetical, conjectural.
Employ	x	Discharge, jobless, dismiss.

Employment	x	Leisure, avocation, unemployment.
Empower	x	Prevent, disqualify, prohibit.
Empty	x	Full, occupied, complete.
Emulation	x	Stagnation, inactivity, dullness.
Enable	x	Weaken, disqualify, incapacitate.
Enact	x	Abolish, repeal, revoke.
Enamor	x	Disenchant, repel, displease.
Encamp	x	Eject, decamp, evict.
Enchain	x	Unfasten, liberate, disconnect.
Enchant	x	Annoy, disgust, repel.
Enchantment	x	Disenchant, repulsion, offensiveness.
Enclosure	x	Open, space, clearing.
Encomium	x	Censure, correction, blame.
Encounter	x	Evade, avoidance, surrender.
Encourage	x	Discourage, dishearten, deter.
Encroach	x	Give, ignore, refrain.
Encumber	x	Aid, assist, alleviate.
Encumbrance	x	Aid, advantage, benefit.

End	x	Beginning, continuation, preface.
Endanger	x	Guard, protect, shield, save.
Endear	x	Disconnect, dislike, hate.
Endeavor	x	Neglect, idleness, inactivity.
Endless	x	Ceasing, mortal, temporary.
Endow	x	Dis-endow, decrease, defund.
Endowment	x	Debt, drawback, disability.
Endure	x	Dismiss, reject, disallow.
Enemy	x	Friend, ally, associate.
Energetic	x	Dull, lethargic, dispirited.
Energy	x	Indolence, laziness, lethargic.
Enervate	x	Invigorate, brace, stimulate.
Enfeeble	x	Strengthen, invigorate, rejuvenate.
Enfold	x	Exclude, unwrap, reveal.
Enforce	x	Disregard, ignore, waive.
Enforcement	x	Renunciation, abandon, neglect.
Enfranchise	x	Bind, confine, enchain.
Engage	x	Elude, escape, retreat.

Engagement	x	Disengagement, breach, removal.
Engaging	x	Repellent, boring, unexciting.
Engender	x	Cease, abolish, destroy.
Engrave	x	Erase, expunge, obliterate.
Engross	x	Bore, tire, distract.
Enhance	x	Worsen, damage, neglect.
Enigmatic	x	Intelligible, accessible, explicit.
Enjoin	x	Relinquish, yield, obey.
Enjoy	x	Dislike, hate, abandon.
Enjoyable	x	Boring, dull, hellish.
Enjoyment	x	Depression, gloom, discontent.
Enlarge	x	Contract, diminish, compress.
Enlighten	x	Mislead, misinform, confuse.
Enlist	x	Demit, withdraw, dismiss.
Enliven	x	Depress, dampen, weaken.
Enmity	x	Friendship, amiability, amity.
Ennoble	x	Condemn, degrade, denounce.
Enormity	x	Righteous, smallness, delight.

Enormous	x	Trivial, miniature, common.
Enough	x	Insufficient, inadequate, partially.
Enrage	x	Soothe, calm, delight.
Enrapture	x	Distress, oppress, bore.
Enrich	x	Damage, deface, decrease.
Enroll	x	Exclude, delist, reject.
Enshrine	x	Condemn, defile, degrade.
Enslave	x	Free, release, alienate.
Ensue	x	Precede, cause, neglect.
Entail	x	Exclude, untangle, untwist.
Entangle	x	Disentangle, unknot, clarify.
Enter	x	Leave, depart, exit.
Enterprise	x	Idleness, monotony, inactivity.
Enterprising	x	Unambitious, timid, cautious, cowardly.
Entertain	x	Annoy, bore, disturb.
Entertainment	x	Disturbance, dissatisfaction, melancholy.
Enthrone	x	Dethrone, debase, degrade.

Enthusiasm	x	Apathy, indifference, lethargy.
Entice	x	Repel, alert, caution.
Entire	x	Deficient, partial, incomplete.
Entitle	x	Disable, disqualify, disallow.
Entity	x	Nonentity, abstract, inanimate.
Entomb	x	Exhume, unearth, disinter.
Entrance	x	Exit, ejection, expulsion.
Entreat	x	Intimate, suggest, oblige.
Entry	x	Exit, conclusion, dismissal.
Entwine	x	Straighten, disentwine, untwist.
Enumerate	x	Conceal, estimate, hide.
Enunciate	x	Confine, suppress, mumble.
Envelop	x	Expose, reveal, free.
Envenom	x	Endear, appease, sweeten.
Envious	x	Unenvious, friendly, contented.
Environ	x	Free, release, unloose.
Envy	x	Benevolence, admiration, loving.
Ephemeral	x	Enduring, perpetual, unceasing.

Epigrammatic	x	Pleonastic, redundant, diffuse.
Epitome	x	Expansion, extension, amplification.
Equable	x	Harsh, inclement, severe.
Equal	x	Dissimilar, unequal, unlike.
Equality	x	Inequality, imparity, difference.
Equality	x	Dissimilarity, difference, inequality.
Equanimity	x	Agitation, excitement, perturbation.
Equip	x	Deprive, dispossess, deprive.
Equitable	x	Biased, inequitable, prejudiced.
Equity	x	Inequity, injustice, dishonesty.
Equivalent	x	Unequal, different, uneven.
Equivocal	x	Certain, evident, clear.
Eradicate	x	Conserve, restore, create.
Erase	x	Record, imprint, engrave.
Erect	x	Prostrate, flat, slant.
Err	x	Forgive, repent, obey.
Erratic	x	Constant, steady, methodical.
Erring	x	Virtuous, forgive, repent.

Erroneous	x	Correct, accurate, exact.
Error	x	Accuracy, correctness, perfection.
Erudition	x	Ignorance, illiteracy, stupidity.
Eruption	x	Implosion, trickle, consumption.
Escape	x	Custody, detention, stay.
Esoteric	x	Shallow, superficial, simple.
Essence	x	Abstract, exterior, outside.
Essential	x	Inessential, incidental, optional.
Establish	x	Disestablish, disprove, prevent.
Estate	x	Disorder, disrepair, waste.
Esteem	x	Condemnation, disregard, disapproval.
Estimable	x	Disreputable, inestimable, dishonourable.
Eternal	x	Ephemeral, mortal, momentary.
Etiquette	x	Discourtesy, indecency, impoliteness.
Euphonious	x	Harsh, discordant, lyrical.
Euphuism	x	Conciseness, Simplicity, bluntness.
Evacuate	x	Fill, load, keep.

Evaporate	x	Emerge, appear, arrive.
Evasion	x	Directness, endurance, abidance.
Even	x	Uneven, rough, varying.
Event	x	Cessation, idleness, inactivity.
Eventful	x	Insignificant, unimportant, inconsequential.
Ever	x	Never, nevermore, once.
Everlasting	x	Ephemeral, impermanent, temporary.
Every	x	None, neither, no one.
Evict	x	Reinstate, admit, hold.
Evidence	x	Dis-proof, rebuttal, concealment.
Evince	x	Conceal, misrepresent, suppress.
Evoke	x	Repress, ignore, disregard.
Exactly	x	Inexactly, imprecisely, partially.
Exaggerate	x	Understate, belittle, contract.
Examine	x	Skim, approve, forget.
Excavate	x	Cover, fill, bury.
Except	x	Approve, sanction, include.
Exception	x	Acceptance, admittance, allowance.

Exceptionable	x	Unobjectionable, inoffensive, acceptable.
Exceptional	x	Common, frequent, familiar.
Excess	x	Scarcity, deficient, meager.
Excessive	x	Insufficient, scant, inadequate.
Excitability	x	Immobility, apathy, calmness.
Excite	x	Allay, bore, deject.
Exclude	x	Include, embrace, admit.
Exclusive	x	Inclusive, nonexclusive, pooled.
Excommunicate	x	Admit, accept, include.
Excrescence	x	Adornment, decoration, enhancement.
Excrete	x	Absorb, accept, allow.
Excruciate	x	Abet, assist, comfort.
Exculpate	x	Accuse, blame, charge.
Excuse	x	Charge, condemn, convict.
Execrable	x	Excellent, fine, choice.
Execration	x	Benediction, blessing, citation.
Execute	x	Disregard, neglect, create.

Exemplary	x	Low-grade, poor, unworthy.
Exemplify	x	Confuse, conceal, obscure.
Exempt	x	Non-exempt, accountable, responsible.
Exemption	x	Liability, responsibility, exposure.
Exercise	x	Disuse, inaction, idleness.
Exertion	x	Entertainment, inaction, facility.
Exhalation	x	Inhalation, exsiccation, absorption.
Exhale	x	Inhale, breathe in, inspire.
Exhaust	x	Activate, energize, renew.
Exhibit	x	Conceal, hide, suppress.
Exhilarate	x	Bore, tire, animate.
Exhort	x	Dissuade, deter, discourage.
Exigency	x	Advantage, benefit, blessing.
Exile	x	Repatriation, return, inclusion.
Existence	x	Inexistence, non-being, abstract.
Exit	x	Entrance, approach, coming.
Expand	x	Contract, compress, abbreviate.
Expanse	x	Extreme, limitation, confine.

Expatiate	x	Compress, decrease, reduce.
Expect	x	Doubt, neglect, question.
Expectation	x	Disbelief, distrust, despair.
Expected	x	Unexpected, untimely, premature.
Expediency	x	Imprudence, inexpediency, inadvisability.
Expedition	x	Blockage, hindrance, delay.
Expel	x	Hold, admit, accept.
Expend	x	Accumulate, save, hoard.
Expense	x	Asset, income, profit.
Expensive	x	Cheap, inexpensive, moderate.
Experience	x	Inexperience, ignorance, immaturity.
Experiment	x	Abstention, neglect, inaction.
Experimental	x	Non-experimental, unproven, tested.
Explain	x	Obscure, confound, mystify.
Explanation	x	Confusion, misinterpretation, mystification.
Explicit	x	Implicit, ambiguous, inexact.
Exponent	x	Antagonist, adversary, opponent.

Export	x	Import, retain, hold.
Exposed	x	Unexposed, covered, protected.
Expostulate	x	Approve, accept, sanction.
Express	x	Suppress, implicit, conceal.
Expression	x	Suppression, question, concealment.
Expunge	x	Conserve, create, repair.
Exquisite	x	Feeble, careless, indelicate.
Extemporaneous	x	Deliberate, intentional, premeditated.
Extend	x	Contract, abbreviate, abridge.
Extenuate	x	Develop, expand, enhance.
Exterior	x	Interior, central, middle.
Exterminate	x	Conserve, protect, bear.
Extermination	x	Rescue, erection, construction.
External	x	Internal, inborn, native.
Extinction	x	Preservation, erection, restoration.
Extinguish	x	Ignite, light, start.
Extort	x	Forfeit, give, loosen.
Extract	x	Insertion, refusal, incorporate.

Extraneous	x	Intrinsic, inherent, essential.
Extraordinary	x	Common, average, ordinary.
Extravagance	x	Economy, moderation, frugality.
Extravagant	x	Miserly, conserving, frugal.
Extreme	x	Intermediate, innermost, middle.
Extremity	x	Beginning, commencement, aid.
Extrovert	x	Introvert, wallflower, introversive.
Exudation	x	Assignment, delegation, hiring.
Exude	x	Absorb, conceal, surge.
Exult	x	Grieve, bemoan, regret.
Exultant	x	Depressed, disappointed, mournful.
Exultation	x	Grief, mourning, depression.

F

Fable	x	Fact, actuality, non-fiction.
Fabricate	x	Destroy, demolish, imitate.
Fabulous	x	Actual, factual, authentic.
Face	x	Avoid, doubt, uncertainty.
Facetious	x	Formal, serious, sincere.
Facile	x	Arduous, profound, complicated.
Facility	x	Hardship, disinclination, discomfort.
Fact	x	Fiction, error, fallacy.
Factious	x	Accommodating, genial, agreeable.
Factitious	x	Authentic, artless, effortless.
Fade	x	Appear, arrive, brighten.
Fag	x	Drone, Idler, freshen.
Fail	x	Pass, ascend, rise.

Failure	x	Success, victory, improvement.
Faint	x	Strong, powerful, bright.
Fair	x	Unfair, biased, ugly.
Faith	x	Disbelief, doubt, atheism.
Faithful	x	Unfaithful, disloyal, unreliable.
Fake	x	Genuine, authentic, legitimate.
Fall	x	Rise, ascent, climb.
Fallacy	x	Truth, accuracy, honesty.
Fallible	x	Infallible, certain, perfect.
Fallow	x	Active, functional, vigorous.
Falsehood	x	Frankness, truthfulness, genuineness.
Falsify	x	Verify, prove, confirm.
Falter	x	Advance, plunge, proceed.
Fame	x	Anonymity, obscurity, unpopularity.
Familiar	x	Unfamiliar, unacquainted, seldom.
Famine	x	Abundance, plenty, wealth.
Famous	x	Notorious, infamous, forgotten.
Fanatic	x	Conservative, unbeliever, moderate.
Fanaticism	x	Apathy, calmness, impartiality.

Fanciful	x	Realistic, sensible, actual.
Fancy	x	Fact, modest, unadorned.
Fantasy	x	Reality, actuality, fact.
Far	x	Near, abrupt, close.
Farcical	x	Grave, serious, reasonable.
Fare	x	Bane, toxin, poison.
Farewell	x	Salutation, welcome, greeting.
Farther	x	Nearer, fewer, closer.
Fascination	x	Repulsion, disinterestness, offensiveness.
Fashion	x	Debasement, disorganization, departure.
Fashionable	x	Unfashionable, dull, outmoded.
Fast	x	Slow, sluggish, loose.
Fasten	x	Unfasten, detach, disconnect.
Fastidious	x	Un-fastidious, uncritical, undemanding.
Fat	x	Lean, slender, emaciated.
Fatal	x	Beneficial, providential, harmless.
Fathom	x	Misunderstand, misinterpret, overlook.
Fathomless	x	Fathomable, infinite, shallow.

Fatigue	x	Freshness, invigorate, rejuvenate.
Fatuity	x	Prudence, discretion, sense.
Fault	x	Accuracy, perfection, success.
Faultless	x	Defective, faulty, guilty.
Faulty	x	Faultless, perfect, accurate.
Favor	x	Disoblige, disfavor, disapprove.
Favorable	x	Unfavorable, adverse, unfriendly.
Favoritism	x	Impartiality, fairness, justice.
Fealty	x	Alienation, disloyalty, disaffection.
Fear	x	Courage, assurance, boldness.
Fearful	x	Fearless, adventuresome, bold.
Feasible	x	Impractical, unrealistic, impossible.
Feast	x	Starvation, barrenness, deficiency.
Featly	x	Awkward, clumsily, bungling.
Feature	x	Whole, lack, miss.
Federation	x	Separation, division, antagonism.
Feeble	x	Strong, mighty, capable.
Feed	x	Famish, starve, diet.
Feeling	x	Callousness, apathy, insensitiveness.

Felicitation	x	Condolence, deprecate, diminish.
Felicitous	x	Dull, inauspicious, annoying.
Felicity	x	Affliction, agony, impropriety.
Fell	x	Beneficial, alleviate, rise.
Fellow	x	Enemy, opponent, antagonist.
Fellowship	x	Rivalry, aloofness, forlornness.
Felonious	x	Lawful, ethical, approved.
Feminine	x	Unfeminine, masculine, accented.
Fence	x	Opening, entrance, doorway.
Ferment	x	Order, calm, orderliness.
Fertile	x	Barren, unfertile, unproductive.
Fertility	x	Infertility, sterility, emptiness.
Festive	x	Abject, aggrieved, miserable.
Fetid	x	Ambrosial, aromatic, scented.
Fetter	x	Free, advantage, benefit.
Feud	x	Accord, harmony, friendship.
Fever	x	Calmness, fitness, health.
Few	x	Majority, abundance, plenty.
Fiber	x	Indecisiveness, cowardice, cravenness.

Fickle	x	Firm, abiding, constant, stable.
Fiction	x	Non-fiction, actuality, fact.
Fictitious	x	Real, authentic, genuine.
Fidelity	x	Infidelity, disloyalty, alienation.
Field	x	Circumscription, constraint, exclusion.
Fierce	x	Docile, amicable, gentle.
Fiery	x	Affable, cold, detached.
Fight	x	Truce, concord, pacification.
Figurative	x	Literal, non-figurative, non-symbolic.
Fill	x	Drain, empty, vacate.
Filter	x	Begrime, contaminate, pollute.
Filthy	x	Clean, decent, acceptable.
Final	x	First, beginning, adjustable.
Find	x	Lose, misplace, miss.
Fine	x	Rough, coarse, adulterated.
Finery	x	Disarray, rags, tatters.
Finical	x	Affable, breezy, understanding.
Finish	x	Start, baseline, continuation.
Finite	x	Infinite, unlimited, unbounded.

Firmness	x	Infirmity, indecision, instability.
First	x	Final, auxiliary, secondary.
Fit	x	Unfit, unqualified, impractical.
Fitful	x	Constant, changeless, stable.
Fix	x	Unfix, break, unsettle.
Flaccid	x	Firm, inflexible, brittle.
Flagitious	x	Good, innocent, lawful
Flaring	x	Appropriate, mute, conservative.
Flat	x	Absorbing, active, upright.
Flattery	x	Detraction, belittlement, blame.
Flaunt	x	Conceal, disguise, cover.
Flavor	x	Classic, tastelessness, inodorousness.
Flexible	x	Rigid, inflexible, harsh.
Flicker	x	Blackness, gloom, float.
Flimsy	x	Solid, probable, sturdy.
Flinch	x	Advance, stay, confront.
Fling	x	Snatch, bring, carry.
Flippant	x	Earnest, sincere, mannerly.
Float	x	Sink, drown, settle.

Flock	x	Disperse, scatter, separate.
Flood	x	Drought, drain, dearth.
Florid	x	Plain, austere, ashy.
Flounder	x	Breeze, glide, slide.
Flourish	x	Flounder, fail, decline.
Flow	x	Clot, flounder, end.
Flower	x	Decay, decline, fade.
Flowing	x	Dry, clotted, empty.
Fluctuate	x	Abide, persist, remain.
Flurry	x	Calm, slump, trickle.
Flutter	x	Steady, calm, remain.
Flux	x	Exodus, outflow, outpouring.
Focus	x	Blear, exterior, periphery.
Foggy	x	Clear, definite, bright.
Foible	x	Excellence, merit, advantage.
Foil	x	Abet, advance, promote.
Fold	x	Unfold, spread, individualist.
Follow	x	Antedate, precede, disobey.
Follower	x	Adversary, antagonist, leader.

Folly	x	Carefulness, wisdom, prudence.
Foment	x	Bridle, check, constrain.
Fond	x	Averse, unloving, unaffectionate.
Fondle	x	Disbelieve, release, maltreat.
Fondness	x	Animosity, hatred, aversion.
Fool	x	Briny, intelligent, genius.
Foolish	x	Wise, rational, realistic.
Footing	x	Dislodgment, ousting, unstableness.
Foray	x	Absenteeism, idleness, laziness.
Forbear	x	Acquiesce, concede, accept.
Forbid	x	Allow, add, admit.
Forbidding	x	Agreeable, begin, gentle.
Force	x	Weakness, agreement, consent.
Fore	x	Aft, dorsal, after.
Forefather	x	Descendants, lineage, successor.
Forego	x	Adopt, complete, succeed.
Foreign	x	Native, domestic, aboriginal.
Forerunner	x	Descendent, offshoot, successor.
Foresee	x	Misinterpret, overlook, neglect.

Foretell	x	Recite, narrate, assure.
Forethought	x	Carelessness, despair, shortsightedness.
Forever	x	Never, infrequently, rarely.
Forfeit	x	Claim, award, gain.
Forge	x	Destroy, demolish, remain.
Forgery	x	Original, honesty, reality.
Forget	x	Remember, accomplish, remind.
Forgetful	x	Alert, attentive, careful.
Forgetfulness	x	Alertness, awareness, attentiveness.
Forgotten	x	Remembered, reclaimed, redeemed.
Forlorn	x	Accompanied, attended, cheered.
Form	x	Formless, disorder, dismantle.
Form	x	Deform, decompose, decay.
Formal	x	Informal. irregular, inaccurate.
Formalism	x	Simplicity, impoliteness, impropriety.
Formality	x	Informality, unconventionality, originality.
Former	x	Later, after, advanced.
Formidable	x	Calm, accessible, achievable.

Forthwith	x	Hereafter, slowly, later.
Fortify	x	Weaken, dismantle, damage.
Fortitude	x	Apathy, cowardice, indecisiveness.
Fortuitous	x	Anticipated, calculated, deliberate.
Fortunate	x	Unfortunate, inopportune, untimely.
Fortune	x	Misfortune, ill luck, accident.
Forward	x	Backward, reversed, careless.
Foul	x	Clean, disinfect, acceptable.
Found	x	Abolish, close, break.
Foundation	x	Top, cowardice, exterior.
Founder	x	Disciple, follower, supporter.
Fraction	x	Whole, total, entirety.
Fragile	x	Compact, tough, hardy.
Fragment	x	Whole, heal, reconstruct.
Fragrant	x	Inodorous, malodorous, bland.
Frail	x	Sturdy, infrangible, mighty.
Frame	x	Centre, disassemble, mishandle.
Franchise	x	Disfranchisement, responsibility, liability.

Frank	x	Secret, abnormal, ambiguous.
Frantic	x	Balanced, composed, calm.
Fraternity	x	Disintegration, isolation, solitude.
Fraternize	x	Avoid, shun, alienate.
Fraud	x	Candidness, sincerity, artlessness.
Fraught	x	Bare, empty, restful.
Freakish	x	Constant, normal, changeless
Free	x	Restricted, accused, caught.
Freedom	x	Slavery, captivity, subjection.
Freeze	x	Unfreeze, boil, heat.
Frenzy	x	Calm, harmony, caution.
Frequent	x	Rare, occasional, intermittent.
Fresh	x	Stale, experienced, old.
Fretful	x	Gentle, calm, obedient.
Friction	x	Accord, agreement, cooperation.
Friend	x	Adversary, enemy, foe.
Friendly	x	Unfriendly, hostile, aloof.
Friendship	x	Enmity, hostility, hatred.
Frighten	x	Assure, comfort, console.

Frightful	x	Pleasing, comforting, beautiful.
Frigid	x	Friendly, ardent, cordial.
Frisk	x	Mope, sulk, stew.
Frisky	x	Apathetic, inactive, depressed.
Fritter	x	Hoard, save, conserve.
Frivolous	x	Intelligent, earnest, sensible.
Frolic	x	Constraint, sadness, obligation.
Frolicsome	x	Clumsy, sullen, staid.
Front	x	Back, after, rear.
Froward	x	Amenable, agreeable, compliant.
Frown	x	Smile, grin, laugh.
Frugal	x	Expensive, bountiful, careless.
Frugality	x	Abundance, extravagance, bounty.
Fruit	x	Antecedent, cause, seed.
Fruitful	x	Fruitless, unproductive, barren.
Fruition	x	Defeat, failure, disappointment.
Frustrate	x	Promote, encourage, aid.
Fugacious	x	Ceaseless, persistent, perpetual.

Fulfill	x	Foil, abandon, neglect.
Full	x	Empty, half, little.
Fully	x	Partially, incompletely, randomly.
Fulminate	x	Grunt, slur, whisper.
Fulsome	x	Inoffensive, reasonable, acceptable.
Fume	x	Calm, moderate, allay.
Function	x	Malfunction, unemployment, inaction.
Fund	x	Defund, draw, debt.
Fundamental	x	Advanced, sophisticated, extensive.
Funny	x	Serious, boring, mournful.
Furbish	x	Rough, scuff, damage.
Furious	x	Calm, cheerful, gentle.
Furnish	x	Conserve, divest, waste.
Furtive	x	Aboveboard, honest, candid
Fuse	x	Diffuse, clot, harden.
Fuss	x	Quiet, acceptance, acclaim.
Futile	x	Effective, fruitful, adequate.
Future	x	Past, ancient, distant.

G

Gag	x	Evoke, provoke, inspire.
Gage	x	Breach, break, uncertainty.
Gaiety	x	Sorrow, dejection, blue.
Gain	x	Loss, deduction, subtraction.
Gainful	x	Disadvantageous, unprofitable, unfavorable.
Gallant	x	Coward, humble, afraid.
Gamesome	x	Dull, depressed, serious.
Garb	x	Bareness, disarray, reality.
Garble	x	Clarify, clear, explain.
Garnish	x	Blemish, blot, decrease.
Garrulity	x	Brevity, briefness, compactness.
Garrulous	x	Quiet, concise, reserved.

Gather	x	Scatter, sow, disperse.
Gaudy	x	Appropriate, modest, conservative.
Gaunt	x	Stout, bright, healthy.
Gawky	x	Graceful, athletic, clever.
Gay	x	Gloomy, unambitious, dull.
Gaze	x	Blink, ignore, glance.
General	x	Particular, specific, uncommon.
Generality	x	Specificity, minority, component.
Generate	x	Impede, restrict, abolish.
Generic	x	Individual, component, exclusive.
Generous	x	Miserly, mean, greedy.
Genial	x	Morose, disagreeable, depressed.
Genius	x	Dunce, stupidity, ignorance.
Genteel	x	Uncivilized, arrogant, barbaric.
Gentle	x	Abrasive, cruel, agitated.
Genuine	x	Spurious, artificial, bogus.
Germane	x	Extraneous, irrelevant, pointless.
Germinate	x	Perish, cease, decay.

Get	x	Abandon, lose, deter.
Ghastly	x	Agreeable, moderate, comforting.
Ghost	x	Angel, God, reality.
Giant	x	Dwarf, little, minute.
Gibe	x	Applaud, compliment, approve.
Giddy	x	Earnest, steady, clearheaded.
Gift	x	Advance, bribe, compensation.
Gigantic	x	Dwarf, insignificant, petty.
Gist	x	Exterior, insignificant, surface.
Give	x	Take, accept, refuse.
Giver	x	Receiver, opponent, opposer.
Glad	x	Sorry, displeased, disappointed.
Gladden	x	Displease, annoy, agitate.
Glare	x	Gloom, dullness, darkness.
Glassy	x	Rough, unglazed, dull.
Glaze	x	Darkness, dullness, stripper.
Glee	x	Dejection, sorrow, depression.
Glimpse	x	Stare, observe, wink.

Gloom	x	Bliss, blaze, glow.
Gloomy	x	Bright, blissful, cheerful.
Glorify	x	Blame, condemn, criticize.
Glorious	x	Inglorious, humble, lowly.
Glory	x	Blemish, disgrace, condemn.
Gloss	x	Dullness, dinginess, dirtiness.
Glowing	x	Dim, dull, apathetic.
Glut	x	Scarcity, deny, check fast.
Gluttony	x	Abstinence, abstemiousness, apathy.
Go	x	Come, halt, malfunction.
Godly	x	Godless, blasphemous, human.
Good	x	Bad, absurd, inferior.
Goodly	x	Bantam, bad, dinky.
Gorgeous	x	Awful, ugly, abhorrent.
Govern	x	Mismanage, abandon, neglect.
Governable	x	Ungovernable, difficult, unmanageable.
Grace	x	Disgrace, gracelessness, blemish.
Graceful	x	Ungraceful, awkward, clumsy.

Graceless	x	Graceful, acceptable, beautiful.
Gracious	x	Discourteous, rude, impolite.
Gradation	x	Equality, accord, unimportance.
Gradual	x	Abrupt, sudden, instantaneous.
Grand	x	Poor, humble, awful.
Grandeur	x	Dullness, insignificance, simplicity.
Grant	x	Confiscate, withdraw, refusal.
Grasp	x	Release, helplessness, abandon.
Grateful	x	Ungrateful, abusive, rude.
Gratification	x	Discontent, agitation, dissatisfaction.
Gratify	x	Aggravate, displease, depress.
Gratitude	x	Ingratitude, thanklessness, ungratefulness.
Gratuitous	x	Essential, costly, compulsory.
Grave	x	Trivial, absurd, petty.
Great	x	Insignificant, amateur, brief.
Greatness	x	Smallness, unimportance, powerless.
Greediness	x	Generosity, benevolence, philanthropy.
Greedy	x	Generous, benevolent, content.

Grief	x	Pleasure, bliss, delight.
Grievance	x	Acclaim, rejoicing, praise.
Grieve	x	Cheer, approve, rejoice.
Grievous	x	Acceptable, bearable, easy.
Grim	x	Agreeable, amiable, light.
Grip	x	Release, misconception, impotency.
Gross	x	Insignificant, lean, skinny.
Grotesque	x	Artful, attractive, aesthetic.
Ground	x	Blunt, dull, flat.
Grounded	x	Afloat, offshore, close.
Groundless	x	Actual, authentic, correct.
Group	x	Dispel, scatter, individual.
Grovel	x	Boast, answer, ignore.
Grow	x	Abide, decay, cease.
Grudge	x	Amiability, friendliness, amity.
Guardian	x	Ward, charge, dependent.
Guess	x	Fact, reality, certainty.
Guest	x	Host, occupant, dweller.

Guide	x	Misguide, follower, cheat.
Guile	x	Forthrightness, frankness, sincerity.
Guilt	x	Guiltless, Blamelessness, innocence.
Guise	x	Disguise, costume, character.
Gush	x	Deluge, drip, drop.
Gust	x	Calm, quiet, tranquility.
Gusto	x	Apathy, lethargy, indolence.

H

Habilitate	x	Disqualify, disrobe, abase
Habit	x	Disinclination, dislike, hate.
Habitual	x	Irregular, unaccustomed, occasional.
Haggard	x	Healthy, plump, chubby.
Hail	x	Ignore, avoid, drip.
Hairy	x	Hairless, restful, calming.
Halcyon	x	Agitated, angry, depressed.
Hale	x	Afflicted, inappropriate, ailing.
Half	x	Full, complete, whole.
Hallow	x	Desecrate, condemn, curse.
Halt	x	Continuation, extension, advance.
Hamper	x	Assist, aid, clear.
Hand	x	Foot, non- possession, employer.

Handle	x	Mishandle, release, abstain.
Handsome	x	Ugly, awkward, graceless.
Handy	x	Cumbersome, inaccessible, handless.
Hang	x	Ascent, recline, rigidity.
Happen	x	Dematerialize, cease, disappear.
Happiness	x	Unhappiness, grief, mourning.
Happy	x	Unhappy, affliction, discontent.
Harangue	x	Acclaim, approval, blessing.
Harass	x	Activate, soothe, aid.
Hard	x	Soft, delicate, weak.
Harden	x	Soften, dilute, cripple.
Hardihood	x	Cowardice, delicacy, indolence.
Hardly	x	Gently, absolutely, frequently.
Hardship	x	Advantage, blessing, opportunity.
Hardy	x	Delicate, calm, afraid.
Harmed	x	Unharmed, benefit, favor.
Harmless	x	Harmful, abusive, poisonous.
Harmonious	x	Antagonistic, discordant, hostile.

Harmony	x	Disharmony, conflict, anarchy.
Harsh	x	Gentle, comfortable, amiable.
Haste	x	Delay, deliberation, inertia.
Hasten	x	Delay, decelerate, halt.
Hasty	x	Slow, careful, deliberate.
Hate	x	Love, affection, devotion.
Hateful	x	Adorable, benevolent, attractive.
Hatred	x	Acceptance, admiration, affection.
Haughtiness	x	Humility, admiration, modesty.
Haughty	x	Meek, lowly, modest.
Have	x	Have-not, want, need.
Havoc	x	Orderliness, conservation, blessing.
Hazard	x	Safety, safeguard, protection.
Hazy	x	Bright, clear, brilliant.
Head	x	Tail, auxiliary, subordinate.
Heal	x	Hurt, damage, cripple.
Healthy	x	Unhealthy, ailing, apathetic.
Heart	x	Animosity, hatred, apathy.

Heartily	x	Abjectly, bleakly, indifferently.
Hearty	x	Apathetic, unhealthy, ailing.
Heat	x	Chill, impassiveness, frigidity.
Heathenish	x	Civilized, polished, cultured.
Heave	x	Depress, decrease, drop.
Heaven	x	Hell, perdition, depression.
Heavenly	x	Awful, earthly, hellish.
Heavy	x	Light, convenient, absorbing.
Hectic	x	Cool, collected, composed.
Heed	x	Disregard, neglect, heedlessness.
Heedful	x	Heedless, careless, absentminded,
Height	x	Depth, base, bottom.
Heighten	x	Abate, decrease, lower.
Heinous	x	Virtuous, excellent, delightful.
Help	x	Constraint, hindrance, blockage.
Hereditary	x	Acquired, non-hereditary, non-heritable.
Heresy	x	Orthodoxy, conformity, belief.
Heretic	x	Orthodox, believer, conformer.

Heroic	x	Un-heroic, humble, cowardly.
Hesitant	x	Resolute, determined, decisive.
Hesitate	x	Determine, decide, abide.
Heterodox	x	Orthodox, conformist, correct.
Heterogeneous	x	Homogeneous, identical, uniform.
Hew	x	Loosen, drop, fall.
Hiatus	x	Linkage, completeness, closing.
Hibernal	x	Summery, autumnal, cheerful.
Hide	x	Reveal, admit, uncover.
Hideous	x	Attractive, acceptable, beautiful.
High	x	Low, inferior, humble.
Hinder	x	Accelerate, facilitate, promote.
Hire	x	Dismiss, displace, sack.
History	x	Future, Fiction, fable.
Hit	x	Miss, failure, disappointment.
Hitch	x	Unhitch, advantage, help.
Hither	x	Thither, near, there.
Hoard	x	Scatter, disperse, cast.

Hoarse	x	Gentle, polite, mellow.
Hoary	x	New, recent, immature.
Hoax	x	Original, honest, give.
Hobby	x	Vocation, entertainment, aversion.
Hold	x	Release, weakness, differ.
Hollow	x	Solid, convex, bulging.
Holy	x	Unholy, abominable, irreligious.
Homage	x	Disloyalty, censure, admonition.
Homely	x	Aesthetic, attractive, beautiful.
Homogeneous	x	Heterogeneous, dissimilar, different.
Honest	x	Dishonest, biased, lying.
Honesty	x	Artifice, dishonesty, corruption.
Honor	x	Dishonor, contempt, blame.
Honorable	x	Dishonorable, atrocious, bad.
Honorary	x	Earned, titular, professional.
Hoot	x	Applause, cheer, murmur.
Hope	x	Despair, disbelief, doubt.
Hopeful	x	Hopeless, pessimistic, unfortunate.

Horizontal	x	Vertical, dissimilar, aslant.
Horrible	x	Attractive, inoffensive, beautiful,
Horror	x	Calm, delight, affection.
Hospitable	x	Inhospitable, unsociable, antisocial.
Host	x	Guest, visitor, parasite.
Hostage	x	Captor, dictator, conqueror.
Hostile	x	Friendly, hospitable, amiable.
Hostility	x	Friendship, affinity, amity.
Hot	x	Cold, unfashionable, ageless.
Huge	x	Tiny, dwarfed, brief.
Human	x	Inhuman, beastly, angelic.
Humane	x	Brutal, callous, abusive.
Humanity	x	Animosity, cruelty, bestiality.
Humanize	x	Dehumanize, degrade, depress.
Humble	x	Bold, aggressive, eminent.
Humid	x	Arid, dry, cool.
Humiliate	x	Exalt, encourage, elevate.
Humility	x	Pride, compliance, egoism.

Humour	x	Seriousness, agony, pathos.
Humorous	x	Serious, witless, boring.
Hurry	x	Delay, slowness; calm.
Hurt	x	Heal, comfort, alleviate.
Hurtful	x	Gratifying, helpful, beneficial.
Hybrid	x	Purebred, inbred, division.
Hygienic	x	Unhygienic, unsterile, unsanitary.
Hypocrisy	x	Uprightness, genuineness, sincerity.
Hypocritical	x	Candid, artless, genuine.
Hypothesis	x	Certainty, proof, assurance.

I

Idea	x	Actuality, fact, reality.
Ideal	x	Actual, non-abstract, material.
Idealism	x	Materialism, insignificance, depression.
Idealistic	x	Practical, optimistic, romantic.
Ideality	x	Concrete, fact, actuality.
Identical	x	Different, another, distant.
Identify	x	Conceal, contrast, confuse.
Identity	x	Difference, alteration, change.
Idiocy	x	Intelligence, prudence, acuteness.
Idiosyncrasy	x	Conformity, sameness, normality.
Idiot	x	Genius, sage, brain.
Idle	x	Active, functional, alive.
Idolize	x	Abhor, abominate, condemn.

Ignoble	x	Noble, aristocratic, dignified.
Ignominious	x	Honorable, respectable, approved.
Ignominy	x	Admiration, esteem, respect.
Ignoramus	x	Brain, egghead, sage.
Ignorance	x	Knowledge, acquaintance, literacy.
Ignorant	x	Learned, educated, expert.
Ignore	x	Consider, appreciate, heed.
Ill	x	Well, healthy, settled.
Illegal	x	Legal, legitimate, authorized.
Illegible	x	Legible, clean, readable.
Illegitimate	x	Legitimate, lawful, legal.
Illicit	x	Lawful, authorized, legal.
Illiterate	x	Literate, educated, lettered.
Illness	x	Wellness, health, fitness.
Illogical	x	Logical, rational, correct.
Illuminate	x	Blacken, darken, becloud.
Illusion	x	Reality, actuality, truth.
Illusive	x	Existent, real, solid.

Illustrate	x	Obscure, complicate, confuse.
Illustrious	x	Insignificant, average, inferior.
Image	x	Original, concrete, difference.
Imagery	x	Prose, statement, fact.
Imaginary	x	Real, actual, existent.
Imagination	x	Reality, dryness, dullness.
Imaginative	x	Unimaginative, accurate, ordinary.
Imagine	x	Demonstrate, ascertain, conclude.
Imbalance	x	Balance, symmetry, correspondence.
Imbecile	x	Precocious, genius, intelligent.
Imbecility	x	Discretion, prudence, acuteness.
Imbibe	x	Eject, discard, abstain.
Imitate	x	Originate, differ, misrepresent.
Imitative	x	Original, genuine, natural.
Immaculate	x	Impure, defective, imperfect.
Immanent	x	Accidental, adventitious, extraneous.
Immaterial	x	Material, physical, corporeal.
Immature	x	Mature, adult, experience.

Immeasurable	x	Bounded, finite, restricted.
Immediate	x	Late, distant, future.
Immediately	x	Later, hereafter, slowly.
Immemorial	x	Recent, modern, current.
Immense	x	Tiny, awful, little.
Immerse	x	Dry, dehydrate, eject.
Immigrant	x	Emigrant, native, citizen.
Immigration	x	Banishment, deportation, exodus.
Immodest	x	Modest, unassuming, humble.
Immoral	x	Moral, decent, ethical.
Immunity	x	Susceptibility, liability, exposure.
Impact	x	Avoidance, failure, amity.
Impair	x	Aid, assist, cure.
Impartial	x	Partial, biased, prejudiced.
Impassioned	x	Passionless, detached, apathetic.
Impatience	x	Patience, calmness, indifference.
Impeach	x	Exonerate, absolve, acquit.
Impediment	x	Assistance, advantage, catalyst.

Impenetrable	x	Penetrable, porous, unsealed.
Impenitent	x	Penitent, apologetic, ashamed.
Imperative	x	Accountable, inessential, dispensable.
Imperfect	x	Perfect, faultless, complete.
Imperial	x	Lowly, humble, common.
Imperious	x	Humble, meek, non-critic.
Impetuous	x	Cautious, calm, apathetic.
Implement	x	Disregard, neglect, exempt.
Implicate	x	Disconnect, extricate, acquit.
Implication	x	Proof, reality, measurement.
Implicit	x	Explicit, actual, authentic.
Imply	x	Express, declare, announce.
Impolite	x	Polite, civil, courteous.
Import	x	Export, exterior, insignificant.
Importance	x	Unimportance, pettiness, disadvantage.
Important	x	Unimportant, insignificant, trivial.
Importunate	x	Incidental, noncritical, relaxed.
Importune	x	Appease, comfort, console.

Impose	x	Abate, condone, remove.
Imposing	x	Unimposing, insignificant, humble.
Imposition	x	Frankness, honesty, candor.
Impossible	x	Possible, believable, attainable.
Imposture	x	Frankness, artlessness, honesty.
Impotence	x	Capacity, competence, ability.
Impoverish	x	Enrich, augment, enhance.
Impractical	x	Practical, applicable, accessible.
Impregnable	x	Pregnable, absorbent, breakable.
Impregnate	x	Remove, dehydrate, drain.
Impression	x	Actuality, fact, reality.
Impressive	x	Unimpressive, insignificant, detached.
Improve	x	Decline, decrease, deteriorate.
Improvement	x	Deterioration, collapse, breakdown.
Imprudent	x	Prudent, advisable, cautious.
Impudence	x	Humility, modesty, acceptability.
Impugn	x	Agree, approve, compliment.
Impulse	x	Allergy, averseness, repulse.

Impulsive	x	Deliberate, sensible, cautious.
Impure	x	Pure, chaste, refined.
Impute	x	Disconnect, absolve, deny.
In	x	Out, unstylish, unpopular.
Inability	x	Ability, capacity, competence.
Inaccessible	x	Accessible, acquirable, attainable.
Inaccurate	x	Accurate, perfect, correct.
Inactive	x	Active, functional, operative.
Inane	x	Significant, bright, meaningful.
Inanition	x	Closure, capacity, significance.
Inaugurate	x	Cease, abolish, close.
Inauguration	x	Discharge, conclusion, valediction.
Inauspicious	x	Auspicious, favourable, fortunate.
Incandescence	x	Lethargy, blackness, apathy.
Incapable	x	Capable, expert, able.
Incense	x	Depreciation, stink, odor.
Incentive	x	Deterrent, disincentive, counterincentive.
Inception	x	Cessation, closure, conclusion.

Incessant	x	Discontinuous, bounded, alternate.
Inclemency	x	Clemency, mildness, informality.
Inclement	x	Balmy, bright, merciful.
Inclination	x	Declination, antipathy, aversion.
Incline	x	Decline, receding, fall.
Include	x	Exclude, ban, omit.
Inclusive	x	Exclusive, circumscribed, narrow.
Income	x	Expenditure, charge, debt.
Incomplete	x	Complete, adequate, entire.
Incongruous	x	Appropriate, fortunate, compatible.
Inconsistent	x	Consistent, certain, changeless.
Incorrect	x	Correct, accurate, informed.
Increase	x	Decrease, decline, abate.
Inculcate	x	Deprive, neglect, clear.
Incumbent	x	Optional, elective, voluntary.
Incur	x	Forfeit, loose, discourage.
Incursion	x	Defense, repulsion, retreat.
Indebted	x	Unobligated, ungrateful, unappreciative.

Indecent	x	Decent, acceptable, correct.
Indeed	x	Doubtfully, indefinite, dubiously.
Indefatigable	x	Idle, indifferent, indolent,
Indefinite	x	Definite, bounded, limited.
Indelible	x	Forgettable, eradicable, unremarkable.
Indemnify	x	Keep, loose, take.
Independence	x	Slavery, inaptitude, subjection.
Independent	x	Dependent, subordinate, subservient.
Indicate	x	Conceal, announce, declare.
Indication	x	Answer, solution, misinformation.
Indifference	x	Attention, concern, agitation.
Indifferent	x	Attentive, caring, biased.
Indigent	x	Affluent, comfortable, prosperous.
Indignation	x	Amiability, calmness, delight.
Indignity	x	Acclaim, accolade, approval.
Indiscriminate	x	Discriminate, homogeneous, alike.
Indisposed	x	Disposed, eager, happy.
Individual	x	General, common, combined.

Individuality	x	Commonality, non-entity, normality.
Indolence	x	Ambition, diligence, industry.
Indomitable	x	Feeble, beatable, flexible.
Indoor	x	Outdoor, alien, exterior.
Indorse	x	Baffle, frustrate, interfere.
Induce	x	Deter, destroy, restrain.
Induction	x	Deduction, discharge, removal.
Indulge	x	Abstain, deny, deprive.
Indulgence	x	Basic, essential, disapproval.
Indulgent	x	Inconsiderate, abstinent, inflexible.
Industrious	x	Lazy, idle, lethargic.
Industry	x	Idleness, negligence, laziness.
Ineffable	x	Definable, communicable, imaginable.
Inert	x	Active, able, occupied.
Inevitable	x	Avoidable, uncertain, avertable.
Inexpensive	x	Expensive, costly, premium.
Infamous	x	Famous, honorable, reputable.
Infamy	x	Esteem, credit, admiration.

Infant	x	Adult, elder, senior.
Infantile	x	Mature, cosmopolitan, adult.
Infatuation	x	Dislike, hate, hatred.
Infection	x	Sanitation, sterility, disinfection.
Infectious	x	Antiseptic, non-communicable, harmless.
Infer	x	Announce, declare, abstain.
Inference	x	Fact, proof, reality.
Inferior	x	Superior, senior, major.
Inferiority	x	Superiority, seniority, excellence.
Infernal	x	Angelic, godlike, moral.
Infidel	x	Believer, devotee, theist.
Infidelity	x	Fidelity, allegiance, faithfulness.
Infinite	x	Brief, bounded, finite.
Infinitesimal	x	Astronomical, huge, significant.
Infirm	x	Robust, strong, mighty.
Infirmity	x	Fitness, health, perfection.
Inflame	x	Allay, appease, douse.
Inflate	x	Deflate, abridge, compress.

Inflated	x	Deflated, reasonable, shrunken.
Inflection	x	Monotone, straightness, directness.
Inflict	x	Hold, spare, take.
Infliction	x	Remission, sparing, pleasure.
Influence	x	Deter, discourage, hinder.
Influential	x	Anonymous, inconspicuous, inferior.
Inform	x	Misinform, contradict, hide.
Informal	x	Formal, ceremonial, official.
Information	x	Concealment, ignorance, question.
Infringe	x	Comply, conform, obey.
Infuse	x	Deprive, eliminate, clear.
Ingenious	x	Imitative, uncreative, dull.
Ingenuity	x	Dryness, clumsiness, awkwardness.
Ingenuous	x	Disingenuous, critical, deceitful.
Ingratiate	x	Deter, disgust, offend.
Ingredient	x	Admixture, whole, compound.
Inhale	x	Exhale, expire, peck.
Inherent	x	Extrinsic, accidental, acquired.

Inherit	x	Acquire, fail, forfeit.
Inheritance	x	Acquisition, purchase, donation.
Inhuman	x	Human, gentle, polite.
Inimical	x	Friendly, beneficial, advantageous.
Iniquity	x	Morality, decency, honesty.
Initiation	x	Termination, discharge, removal.
Initiative	x	Inactivity, apathy, diffidence.
Inject	x	Eject, eliminate, exclude.
Injunction	x	Allowance, appeal, permission.
Injure	x	Cure, benefit, repair.
Injurious	x	Advantageous, beneficial, assisting.
Injury	x	Advantage, amelioration, benefit
Injustice	x	Justice, equity, delight.
Inlet	x	Outlet, egress, departure.
Inmate	x	Visitor, stranger, outsider.
Innate	x	Extrinsic, acquired, accidental.
Inner	x	Outer, exterior, outmost.
Inner	x	Outer, exterior, external.

Innocence	x	Guilt, sinfulness, vulgarity.
Innocuous	x	Adverse, baleful, poisonous.
Innovation	x	Duplicate, stagnation, imitation.
Inoculate	x	Deprive, divest, inject.
Input	x	Output, production, result.
Inquiry	x	Answer, response, ignorance.
Inquisitive	x	Incurious, apathetic, uncurious.
Inroad	x	Retreat, occupation, evacuation.
Insane	x	Sane, composed, intelligent.
Insanity	x	Sanity, clearness, reality.
Inscribe	x	Delete, forget, decode.
Inscrutable	x	Accessible, clear, comprehensive.
Insert	x	Exclude, deduct, eliminate.
Inside	x	Outside, exterior, innermost.
Insidious	x	Harmless, fair, sincere.
Insinuate	x	Announce, reject, conceal.
Insipid	x	Spirited, exciting, appetizing.
Insist	x	Abandon, deny, desert.

Insolence	x	Acceptability, approval, humility.
Insolvent	x	Solvent, wealthy, rich.
Insomnia	x	Sleep, relaxation, drowsiness.
Inspect	x	Overlook, skim, ignore.
Inspiration	x	Discouragement, calmness, dullness.
Instance	x	Dissuasion, principle, statement.
Instant	x	Ago, future, slow.
Instigate	x	Restrain, appease, calm.
Instill	x	Extract, remove, eliminate.
Instinct	x	Inability, reason, experiment.
Instinctive	x	Acquired, logical, reasonable.
Institute	x	Cease, disestablish, destroy.
Instruct	x	Comply, obey, conceal.
Instruction	x	Appeal, question, obedience.
Instrumentality	x	Blockage, hindrance, hurt.
Insufficient	x	Sufficient, adequate, enough.
Insult	x	Praise, approve, compliment.
Insure	x	Endanger, uncover, enfeeble.

Insurgent	x	Obedient, subordinate, patriot.
Insurrection	x	Calm, peace, control.
Intact	x	Imperfect, abbreviated, partial.
Integrate	x	Disarrange, detach, remove.
Integrity	x	Deceit, badness, artifice.
Intellect	x	Ignorance, inability, insanity.
Intellectual	x	Anti-intellectual, ignorant, uncultured.
Intelligence	x	Ignorance, stupidity, artlessness.
Intelligent	x	Unintelligent, imprudent, dull.
Intelligible	x	Ambiguous, inarticulate, incoherent.
Intend	x	Disbelieve, disregard, neglect.
Intense	x	Mild, detached, alleviated.
Intensity	x	Laxity, feebleness, mildness, apathy.
Intent	x	Flexible, absentminded, method.
Intention	x	Aimlessness, discouragement, means.
Intentional	x	Unintentional, casual, accidental.
Inter	x	Disinter, exhume, admit.
Intercede	x	Avoid, disregard, shun.

Intercept	x	Allow, free, forward.
Interdict	x	Accession, toleration, aid.
Interest	x	Bore, annoy, hate.
Interfere	x	Avoid, disregard, advance.
Interior	x	Exterior, outside, public.
Intermediate	x	Abnormal, excessive, distinctive.
Interment	x	Disinterment, exhumation, unearthing.
Intermission	x	Continuity, stretch, action.
Intermit	x	Continue, begin, complete.
Internal	x	External, outer, outside.
Internecine	x	Bloodless, external, incursive.
Interpolate	x	Eject, exclude, deduct.
Interpose	x	Avoid, eject, remove.
Interpret	x	Misrepresent, obscure, confuse.
Interpretation	x	Misinterpretation, complication ignorance.
Interrogate	x	Answer, reply, avoid.
Interrupted	x	Uninterrupted, continue, advance.
Interstice	x	Continuation, closure, solid.

Interval	x	Continuity, progression, closure.
Intervention	x	Nonintervention, avoid, disregard.
Interview	x	Silence, report, exclusion.
Intestate	x	Testate, willed, devised.
Intimate	x	Aloof, distant, announce.
Intimidate	x	Comfort, assure, cheer.
Intolerable	x	Acceptable, tolerable, deficient.
Intolerant	x	Tolerant, abiding, extreme.
Intoxication	x	Depression, sorrow, abstinence.
Intrepid	x	Afraid, diffident, anxious.
Intricacy	x	Plainness, homogeneous, simplicity.
Intricate	x	Apparent, modest, simple.
Intrigue	x	Honesty, dislike, truthfulness.
Intrinsic	x	Extrinsic, acquired, accidental.
Introduce	x	Abolish, conceal, nullify.
Introduction	x	Conclusion, postscript, close.
Introductory	x	Concluding, advanced, valedictory.
Intrude	x	Avoid, erase, ignore.

Intrusion	x	Defense, retreat, removal,
Intuition	x	Reason, ignorance, acquirement.
Inundate	x	Drain, dry, dehydrate.
Invade	x	Defend, protect, abandon.
Invalid	x	Valid, fit, legitimate.
Invalidate	x	Validate, legislate, establish.
Invasion	x	Defense, surrender, defeat.
Invective	x	Praise, acclaim, courteous.
Invent	x	Clone, duplicate, destroy.
Inventive	x	Uncreative, dull, derivative.
Inventor	x	Copier, imitator, destroyer.
Invert	x	Restore, continue, hold.
Invest	x	Withdraw, divest, deprive.
Investigate	x	Answer, forget, guess.
Investigation	x	Discovery, answer, neglect.
Investiture	x	Divestiture, removal, completion.
Inveterate	x	Intermittent, occasional, brief.
Invidious	x	Generous, delightful, impartial.

Invigorate	x	Blunt, bore, dampen.
Invisible	x	Visible, noticeable, conspicuous.
Invitation	x	Answer, denial, refusal.
Invite	x	Repel, discourage, dispel.
Invoke	x	Restrict, answer, impede.
Involution	x	Simplicity, plainness, homogeneity
Involve	x	Exclude, band, explicate.
Inward	x	Outward, aloof, exterior.
Iota	x	Lot, aggregate, mass.
Irate	x	Delighted, calm, accepting.
Ire	x	Calmness, comfort, amiability.
Irrational	x	Rational, logical, sound.
Irregular	x	Regular, constant, steady.
Irrelevant	x	Relevant, appropriate, applicable.
Irreligious	x	Religious, devout, godly.
Irreparable	x	Reparable, mendable, correctable.
Irresistible	x	Resistible, avoidable, ineffective.
Irresponsible	x	Responsible, careful, accountable.

Irreversible	x	Reversible, correctable, fixable.
Irritable	x	Sooth, pleasant, cordial.
Irritating	x	Pleasant, soothing, silky.
Isolate	x	Attach, integrate, socialite.
Isolation	x	Association, company, fellowship.
Issue	x	Cause, agreement, antecedent.
Itinerant	x	Immobile, settled, permanent.

J

Jade	x	Absorb, engage, activate.
Jagged	x	Aligned, continuous, clean.
Jangle	x	Calm, harmony, order.
Jar	x	Agree, assist, delight.
Jaundiced	x	Generous, affable, unbiased.
Jaunty	x	Gloomy, inanimate, depressed.
Jealous	x	Genial, content, generous.
Jealousy	x	Benevolence, goodwill, generousness.
Jeer	x	Compliment, praise, cheer.
Jejune	x	Absorbing, engaging, mature.
Jeopardy	x	Safety, assurance, defense.
Jest	x	Gravity, earnest, favourite.
Job	x	Jobless, avocation, unemployment.

Jocose	x	Abject, aggrieved, discontented.
Jocund	x	Sad, melancholy, aggrieved.
Join	x	Disjoin, abstain, leave.
Joint	x	Disunited, exclusive, divided.
Jollification	x	Dejection, blackness, dolefulness.
Jolly	x	Gloomy, sad, depressed.
Jostle	x	Repress, clear, pull.
Jot	x	Aggregate, entirely, mass.
Journey	x	Inaction, break, stay.
Jovial	x	Morose, gloomy, depressed.
Joviality	x	Depression, dullness, sadness.
Joy	x	Sorrow, grief, melancholy.
Joyful	x	Sorrowful, depressed, gloomy.
Jubilant	x	Despondent, rejected, dispirited.
Judgment	x	Actuality, fact, ignorance.
Judicial	x	Non-judicial, illegal, uncritical.
Judicious	x	Injudicious, imprudent, careless.
Juggle	x	Expose, undeceive, reveal.

Juicy	x	Obtuse, dry, unexciting.
Jumble	x	Segregate, order, agreement.
Jump	x	Disadvantage, liability, check.
Junction	x	Detachment, disunion, analysis.
Jungle	x	Oder, arrangement, system.
Junior	x	Senior, advanced, greater.
Jurisdiction	x	Exemption, independence, impotence.
Just	x	Unjust, inaccurate, imprecise.
Justice	x	Injustice, corruption, dishonesty.
Justification	x	Censure, charge, indictment.
Justify	x	Condemn, reverse, attack.
Justness	x	Incorrect, irrelevant, unfair.
Juvenile	x	Senile, mature, experienced.
Juxtaposition	x	Distance, remoteness, separateness.

K

Keen	x	Blunt, absurd, apathetic.
Keep	x	Release, displace, damage.
Keeping	x	Dispossession, neglect, abandonment.
Ken	x	Ignorance, misconception, blindness.
Kernel	x	Exterior, periphery, whole.
Key	x	Insignificant, additional, unimportant.
Kick	x	Acceptance, approval, caress.
Kill	x	Breed, animate, create.
Kin	x	Ancestry, unrelated, decent.
Kind	x	Unkind, merciless, cruel.
Kindle	x	Extinguish, put out, douse.
Kindly	x	Unkindly, unfriendly, inconsiderate.
Kindness	x	Cruelty, harshness, severity.

Kindred	x	Irrelevant, disagreeable, dissimilar.
Kinetic	x	Static, inanimate, indolent.
King	x	Subject, inferior, subordinate.
Kingly	x	Beggarly, mean, poor.
Knack	x	Ineptness, constraint, inability.
Knave	x	Gentleman, hero, innocent.
Knavish	x	Honourable, virtuous, grave.
Knot	x	Unknot, entity, detaching.
Knotty	x	Plain, easy, simple.
Know	x	Ignore, misapprehend, overlook.
Knowing	x	Unknowing, oblivious, stupid.
Knowledge	x	Ignorance, illiteracy, clumsiness.
Known	x	Unknown, mistake, unfamiliar.

L

Labor	x	Ease, inactivity, laziness.
Labored	x	Easy, clever, graceful.
Laborer	x	Employer, idler, shirker.
Laborious	x	Easy, facile, idle.
Labyrinth	x	Simplicity, ease, order.
Lack	x	Abundance, plenty, sufficiency.
Laconic	x	Elaborate, wordy, circuitous.
Laical	x	Mental, godly, spiritual.
Lame	x	Able, strong, efficient.
Lament	x	Rejoice, exultation, hail.
Language	x	Silence, quiet, standard.
Languid	x	Active, ambitious, mighty.
Languish	x	Build, thrive, gain.

Languor	x	Strength, vigor, ambition.
Lank	x	Firm, hard, solid.
Lapse	x	Accuracy, extension, continuation.
Large	x	Small, dwarf, mean.
Lash	x	Unlash, compliment, soothe.
Lassitude	x	Energy, action, bounce.
Last	x	First, foremost, nearest.
Lasting	x	Transient, temporary, ephemeral.
Late	x	Early, alive, future, antique.
Lately	x	Ago, before, earlier.
Latent	x	Active, functional, apparent.
Lateral	x	Central, direct, primary, immediate.
Latest	x	Oldest, premier, superior.
Latter	x	Former, beginning, first.
Laud	x	Defame, knock, slam.
Laudable	x	Base, contemptible, deplorable.
Laugh	x	Cry, sob, weep.
Laughter	x	Sadness, cry, groan.

Launch	x	Landing, catch, abolish.
Lavish	x	Misery, deficient, moderate.
Law	x	Lawlessness, partiality, disorder.
Lawful	x	Unlawful, Illegal, illegitimate.
Lawless	x	Lawful, order, legitimate.
Lax	x	Strict, alert, careful.
Lay	x	Ordained, professional, sacred.
Lazy	x	Industrious, active, careful.
Lead	x	Follow, mislead, misguide, abandon.
Leader	x	Follower, dependent, subordinate.
Leafy	x	Leafless, barren, depleted.
League	x	Disunion, neutrality, secession.
Lean	x	Fat, plump, chubby.
Leaning	x	Aversion, dislike, allergy.
Leap	x	Walk, dive, run.
Learn	x	Unlearn, forget, ignore.
Learned	x	Unlearned, uneducated, illiterate.
Learner	x	Teacher, ignoramus, master.

Learning	x	Ignorance, illiteracy, revelation.
Least	x	Most, greatest, prominent.
Leave	x	Come, stay, arrive.
Legal	x	Illegal, unlawful, illegitimate.
Legend	x	Fact, history, no-fiction.
Legible	x	Illegible, ambiguous, obscure.
Legitimate	x	Illegitimate, illegal, abnormal.
Leisure	x	Work, exertion, pressure.
Leisurely	x	Hurried, difficult, speedy.
Lend	x	Borrow, retain, receive.
Length	x	Breadth, extreme, unimportant.
Lengthen	x	Shorten, abbreviate, curtail.
Lengthy	x	Brief, short, compact.
Lenient	x	Harsh, merciless, hateful.
Less	x	More, greater, higher.
Lessen	x	Increase, enlarge, accumulate.
Let	x	Hire, prevent, deny.
Lethal	x	Harmless, helpful, beneficial.

Lethargy	x	Alertness, vigor, vitality.
Lettered	x	Unlettered, ignorant, illiterate.
Level	x	Uneven, agitated, upset.
Levity	x	Depression, dejection, earnestness.
Levy	x	Pay, disapprove, remove.
Liable	x	Irresponsible, exempt, covered.
Libel	x	Acclaim, compliment, honor.
Liberal	x	Conservative, mean, intolerant.
Liberate	x	Confine, block, harm.
Libertine	x	Pure, uncorrupt, ethical.
Liberty	x	Captivity, denial, dependence.
License	x	Prohibit, ban, disqualify.
Licentious	x	Chaste, controlled, frigid.
Licit	x	Illegal, illicit, forbidden.
Lie	x	Truth, frankness, honesty.
Lie	x	Rise, stir, move.
Life	x	Death, lethargy, abstract.
Lift	x	Lower, hindrance, decent.

Ligament	x	Fracture, line, whole.
Light	x	Heavy, dark, gloomy.
Like	x	Dislike, different, unlike.
Likelihood	x	Unlikelihood, improbability, difference.
Likely	x	Unlikely, doubtful, incredible.
Likeness	x	Unlikeness, disparity, inequality.
Likewise	x	Contrariwise, opposing, differently.
Liking	x	Dislike, disrelish, hatred.
Limit	x	Expanse, freedom, center.
Limitless	x	Bounded, limited, brief.
Limpid	x	Cloudy, muddy, incomprehensible.
Line	x	Ancestry, inside, issue.
Lineage	x	Ancestor, parent, origin.
Lineament	x	Whole, abnormality, hatred.
Linear	x	Zigzag, crooked, corrupt.
Linger	x	Hurry, forge, Progress, barrel.
Liquid	x	Solid, hard, cloudy.
Listen	x	Ignore, deny, disregard.

Listless	x	Active, alert, ambitious.
Literal	x	Fictional, hypothetical, counterfeit.
Literary	x	Illiteracy, chatty, colloquial.
Lithe	x	Awkward, clumsy, stiff.
Litter	x	Order, catch, gem.
Little	x	Much, abundant, adequate.
Live	x	Dead, asleep, absent.
Livelihood	x	Avocation, starvation, entertainment.
Liveliness	x	Lifelessness, inactivity, dullness.
Lively	x	Lifeless, dull, apathetic.
Living	x	Dead, extinct, inactive.
Load	x	Unload, ace, bit, dab.
Loan	x	Borrow, receive, take.
Loathe	x	Love, admire, desire.
Locate	x	Lose, overlook, misplace.
Lock	x	Unlock, discharge, release.
Locomotion	x	Repose, rest, stoppage.
Lodge	x	Eject, evict, dislodge.

Lofty	x	Low, flat, below.
Logical	x	Illogical, foolish, absurd.
Lonely	x	Accompanied, populous, attended.
Long	x	Short, abbreviated, little.
Longing	x	Dislike, unconcern, indifference.
Loose	x	Fasten, tight, accurate.
Loquacity	x	Backwardness, bashfulness, coldness.
Lordly	x	Humble, modest, bashful.
Lordship	x	Disrespect, subjection, submission.
Lore	x	Ignorance, illiteracy, reality.
Lose	x	Keep, acquire, adopt.
Loss	x	Gain, advantage, success.
Lot	x	Whole, little, single.
Loud	x	Gentle, soft, calm.
Love	x	Hate, abhor, animosity.
Lovely	x	Ugly, unlovely, hateful.
Low	x	High, eminent, abundant.
Lower	x	Higher, superior, elevated.

Lowering	x	Clear, bright, benign.
Lowly	x	Higher, eminent, arrogant.
Loyal	x	Disloyal, faithless, unfaithful.
Loyalty	x	Enmity, alienation, disgrace.
Lucid	x	Ambiguous, clouded, obscure.
Luck	x	Misfortune, accident, disadvantage.
Lucky	x	Unlucky, cursed, hapless.
Lucrative	x	Disadvantageous, unprofitable, fruitless.
Lucre	x	Loss, debt, expensive.
Lucubration	x	Idleness, disdain, disregard.
Ludicrous	x	Earnest, grave, familiar.
Lugubrious	x	Cheerful, blissful, blithe.
Lull	x	Continuation, progress, charge.
Luminous	x	Dark, dull, insignificant.
Lunacy	x	Sanity, intellect, prudence.
Lunatic	x	Balanced, logical, judicial.
Lure	x	Repulsion, alarm, caution.
Lurid	x	Blooming, clear, delightful.

Lurk	x	Appear, rise, emerge.
Luscious	x	Harsh, disagreeable, painful.
Luster	x	Darkness, gloom, dullness.
Lustration	x	Defilement, contamination, infection.
Lustrous	x	Dark, dull, cloudy.
Luxuriant	x	Un luxuriant, dormant, barren.
Luxuriate	x	Abstain, decrease, decline.
Luxurious	x	Austere, ascetic, hard.
Luxury	x	Austerity, economical, necessity.
Lying	x	Truthful, honest, frank.

M

Macabre	x	Pleasing, cheering, attractive.
Macerate	x	Dehydrate, drain, empty.
Machinate	x	Disorganize, forget, blow.
Machination	x	Frankness, honesty, fairness.
Macrocosm	x	Microcosm, nothingness, void.
Macroscopic	x	Microscopic, small, invisible.
Maculate	x	Elevate, honour, pure.
Mad	x	Sane, balanced, calm.
Madden	x	Calm, ally, please.
Made	x	Unmade, unsuccessful, custom.
Madness	x	Sanity, calmness, balance.
Magisterial	x	Submissive, docile, undignified.
Magnanimity	x	Meanness, selfishness, pettiness.

Magnanimous	x	Mean, ignoble, uncharitable.
Magnificent	x	Lowly, humble, common.
Magnify	x	Simplify, belittle, decrease.
Magniloquent	x	Un-rhetorical, terse, simple.
Magnitude	x	Smallness, littleness, triviality.
Maiden	x	Bachelor, final, ultimate.
Maim	x	Cure, fix, restore.
Main	x	Auxiliary, minor, inferior.
Mainly	x	Secondarily, partially, slightly.
Maintain	x	Abandon, disregard, destroy.
Majestic	x	Un majestic, lowly, shabby.
Majority	x	Minority, inferiority, rare.
Make	x	Unmake, abolish, break.
Maker	x	Destroyer, exterminator, annihilator.
Make up	x	Distribute, disperse, demount.
Malady	x	Health, comfort, strength.
Male	x	Female, feminine, unmanly.
Malediction	x	Benediction, blessing, compliment.

Malefactor	x	Angel, innocent, benefactor.
Malevolent	x	Benevolent, friendly, benign.
Malice	x	Friendliness, affection, kindliness.
Malign	x	Benign, benevolent, loving.
Malignity	x	Compassion, love, passion.
Malodorous	x	Fragrant, aromatic, perfumed.
Manacle	x	Aid, advantage, assist.
Manage	x	Mismanage, collapse, leave.
Manageable	x	Unmanageable, untamable, unfeasible.
Manager	x	Employ, worker, subordinate
Mandate	x	Cancel, breach, request.
Mandatory	x	Optional, elective, inessential.
Maneuver	x	Secession, ignorance, inactivity.
Mangle	x	Aid, better, heal.
Manhood	x	Womanhood, femininity, cowardice.
Mania	x	Sanity, apathy, calmness.
Manifest	x	Latent, hidden, illegible.
Manifold	x	Alike, homogeneous, same.

Manly	x	Unmanly, feminine, cowardly.
Mannerism	x	Conformity, sameness, honesty.
Mannerly	x	Rude, arrogant, impolite.
Manufacture	x	Demolish, copy, divide.
Manumission	x	Bondage, enslavement, emancipation.
Manumit	x	Bind, confine, convict.
Many	x	Few, scarce, limited.
Mar	x	Make, adornment, decoration.
Margin	x	Inside, center, heart.
Marine	x	Amphibious, fresh-water, terrestrial.
Marital	x	Non-marital, single, celibate.
Mark	x	Erase, discredit, blank.
Mark	x	Overlook, ignore, omit.
Marriage	x	Divorce, separation, annulment.
Married	x	Unmarried, separated, single.
Marrow	x	Exterior, outside, exteriority.
Marshal	x	Demobilize, disarrange, disorder.
Martial	x	Non-military, Peaceful, un-soldierly

Martyrdom	x	Comfort, happiness, denial.
Marvel	x	Calmness, normality, doom.
Marvelous	x	Unimpressive, familiar normal.
Masculine	x	Un-masculine, feminine, weak.
Mask	x	Unmask, truth, exposure.
Mass	x	Fragment, minority, few.
Massive	x	Slight, humble, light.
Master	x	Servant, pupil, amateur
Mastery	x	Incompetence, ignorance, impotence.
Match	x	Mismatch, concord, imbalance.
Matchless	x	Common, atrocious, mediocre.
Mate	x	Enemy, competitor, single.
Material	x	Immaterial, airy, insignificant.
Matrimony	x	Annulment, divorce, separation.
Matter	x	Answer, solution, abstract.
Mature	x	Immature, raw, childish.
Maudlin	x	Cynical, unsentimental, pragmatic.
Mawkish	x	Calm, unemotional, unadulterated.

Maximum	x	Minimum, least, lowest.
Maze	x	Certainty, assurance, solution.
Meager	x	Abundant, adequate, surplus.
Mean	x	Decent, generous, excess.
Meaningful	x	Meaningless, unexpressive, exterior.
Meanness	x	Nobleness, affection, benevolence.
Measurable	x	Immeasurable, aberration, deviation.
Measure	x	Bulk, extreme, unimportant.
Measureless	x	Circumscribed, finite, limited.
Mechanical	x	Non-mechanical, calculated, intentional.
Meddle	x	Avoid, facilitate, shun.
Meddlesome	x	Unobtrusive, dodging, apathetic.
Mediate	x	Withdraw, extreme, abandon.
Mediation	x	Contention, disagreement, indifference.
Medicament	x	Blockage, harm, hindrance.
Medicate	x	Enliven, harm, infect.
Mediocre	x	Excellent, superior, capital.
Mediocrity	x	Excellence, superiority, brilliance.

Meditate	x	Ignore, execute, neglect.
Medium	x	Excessive, outer, extreme.
Medley	x	Order, harmony, neatness.
Meek	x	Haughty, arrogant, assertive.
Meet	x	Part, inappropriate, unfit.
Melancholy	x	Happiness, cheerful, thrilling.
Mellifluous	x	Disconnected, harsh, un lyrical.
Mellow	x	Abrasive, hard, discordant.
Melodious	x	Discordant, blaring, inharmonious.
Melody	x	Discord, cacophony, disharmony.
Melt	x	Appear, harden, arrive.
Member	x	Whole, composite, entirety.
Memorable	x	Ordinary, unremarkable, insignificant.
Memorial	x	Abusive, dishonorable, oblivion.
Memory	x	Oblivion, forgetfulness, un mindfulness.
Menace	x	Guard, protection, certainty.
Mend	x	Damage, blemish, harm.
Mendacity	x	Frankness, accuracy, truth.

Menial	x	Noble, exciting, arrogant.
Mental	x	Physical, corporeal, balanced.
Mention	x	Disregard, omission, neglect.
Mercantile	x	Noncommercial, un mercantile, unprofitable.
Mercenary	x	Generous, unselfish, charitable.
Merchant	x	Customer, buyer, salesman.
Merciful	x	Cruel, pitiless, harsh.
Mercy	x	Merciless, cruelty, unkind.
Mere	x	Compound, mixed, adulterated.
Meridian	x	Base, bottom, nadir.
Merit	x	Demerit, blemish, defect.
Merry	x	Miserable, gloomy, depressed.
Message	x	Heedlessness, ignorance, silence.
Metaphysical	x	Physical, concrete, natural.
Method	x	Disorder, chaos, disorganization.
Midst	x	Circumference, perimeter, exterior.
Might	x	Weakness, feebleness, impotence.
Mild	x	Wild, harsh, agitated.

Mind	x	Body, delusion, ignorance.
Mindful	x	Unmindful, careless, inattentive.
Mingle	x	Avoid, separate, detach.
Miniature	x	Huge, astronomical, giant.
Minimize	x	Magnify, acclaim, applaud.
Minimum	x	Maximum, largest, greatest.
Minor	x	Major, greater, fatal.
Minority	x	Majority, bulk, large.
Minute	x	Monstrous, consequential, eventful.
Miraculous	x	Average, common, natural.
Misanthropy	x	Belief, certainty, passion.
Misbehave	x	Behave, obey, acquit.
Miscellany	x	Order, group, uniformity.
Mischance	x	Chance, fortune, luck.
Mischief	x	Graveness, advantage, obedience.
Misconduct	x	Conduct, behavior, obedient.
Miser	x	Spendthrift, prodigal, spender.
Miserable	x	Happy, comfortable, happy.

Miserly	x	Lavish, bountiful, generous.
Misery	x	Happiness, contentment, comfort.
Misfortune	x	Fortune, advantage, achievement.
Mislead	x	Guide, undeceive, expose.
Miss	x	Gain, abundance, success.
Mission	x	Avocation, pastime, entertainment.
Mistrust	x	Trust, assurance, certainty.
Misunderstand	x	Understand, appreciate, comprehend.
Misuse	x	Use, application, employment.
Mitigate	x	Aggravate, injure, sharpen.
Mix	x	Separate, component, segregate.
Mob	x	Individual, single, elite.
Mobile	x	Immobile, fixed, non-migrant.
Model	x	Imitation, average, abnormal.
Moderate	x	Immoderate, extreme, excessive.
Modern	x	Ancient, old-fashioned, antique.
Modest	x	Immodest, excessive, extreme.
Modesty	x	Immorality, arrogance, impropriety.

Moist	x	Dry, arid, dehydrated.
Moment	x	Age, aeon, whole.
Momentary	x	Lasting, permanent, lifelong.
Momentous	x	Trivial, inconsequential, partly.
Monogamy	x	Polygamy, antagonism, disunion.
Monologue	x	Dialogue, quiet, silence.
Monopoly	x	Distribution, scattering, sharing.
Monotonous	x	Varied, eventful, absorbing.
Monster	x	Little, bantam, angel.
Monstrous	x	Shapely, beautiful, gentle.
Moral	x	Immoral, corrupt, bodily.
Morbid	x	Healthy, optimistic, cheerful.
More	x	Less, fewer, little.
Morose	x	Jovial, bright, cheerful.
Mortal	x	Immortal, beneficial, non-human
Mortality	x	Immortality, inhumanness, birth.
Most	x	Least, negligibly, marginally.
Motherly	x	Paternal, fatherly, harsh.

Motion	x	Stillness, immobility, rest.
Motionless	x	Mobile, immobility, stillness.
Motive	x	Deterrent, neglect, consequence.
Mount	x	Dismount, decrease, valley.
Mourn	x	Delight, exult, rejoice.
Mournful	x	Cheerful, beaming, blissful.
Movable	x	Immovable, fixed, permanent.
Move	x	Stop, cessation, immobility.
Movement	x	Stoppage, immobility, cessation.
Moving	x	Static, unemotional, stationary.
Much	x	Little, paltry, anonymous.
Multiplication	x	Decrease, subtraction, singularity.
Multiply	x	Divide, diminish, shrink.
Multitude	x	Little, individual, aristocracy.
Mundane	x	Noble, abnormal, celestial.
Munificent	x	Cheap, small, careful.
Musical	x	Unmusical, discordant, cacophonous.
Mute	x	Vocal, communicative, talkative

Mutual	x	Detached, personal, exclusive.
Mysterious	x	Apparent, accessible, clear.
Mystic	x	Physical, intelligible, obvious.
Myth	x	Truth, fact, certainty.

N

Nabob	x	Inferior, subordinate, nobody.
Nadir	x	Zenith, bloom, apex.
Nag	x	Console, please, assist.
Naive	x	Crafty, intelligent, sophisticated.
Naked	x	Clothed, covered, adorned.
Name	x	Obscure, unknown, disreputable.
Narrate	x	Conceal, suppress, foretell.
Narrow	x	Broad, wide, liberal.
Nascent	x	Advanced, developed, dying.
Nasty	x	Clean, pleasant, admirable.
Native	x	Alien, acquired, auxiliary.
Natural	x	Unnatural, cultivated, abnormal.
Nature	x	Nothingness, void, subject.

Naught	x	Achievement, actuality, fulfillment.
Naughty	x	Obedient, behaved, decent.
Nausea	x	Appetite, fondness, relish.
Near	x	Far, distant, absolute.
Nearly	x	Distantly, Scarcely, absolutely.
Neat	x	Dirty, awkward, adulterated.
Nebulous	x	Distinct, accessible, obvious.
Necessary	x	Unnecessary, inessential, optional.
Necessitate	x	Hold, eliminate, calculate.
Necessity	x	Luxury, auxiliary, affluence.
Need	x	Non-essential, amenity, luxury
Needful	x	Undesired, dispensable, needless.
Needless	x	Needful, crucial, essential.
Needy	x	Needless, affluent, prosperous.
Nefarious	x	Lawful, decent, elevated.
Negation	x	Assertion, affirmation, approval.
Negative	x	Positive, affirmative, advantageous.
Neglect	x	Care, attention, regard.

Negotiate	x	Blow, confuse, botch.
Neighborly	x	Alienated, hostile, unfriendly.
Nerve	x	Cowardice, calm, aplomb.
Nervous	x	Valiant, confident, nerveless.
Neutral	x	Partial, affiliated, biased.
Neutralize	x	Raise, restore, enhance.
Never	x	Ever, always, completely.
New	x	Old, antiquated, common.
News	x	Ignorance, question, deceit.
Nice	x	Coarse, improper, disagreeable.
Nicety	x	Inaccuracy, error, burden.
Niggard	x	Spendthrift, bountiful, generous.
Niggardly	x	Abundant, adequate, bountiful.
Nigh	x	Far, away, separated.
Nimble	x	Awkward, absurd, clumsy.
Nobility	x	Commoners, dishonor, serfdom.
Noble	x	Ignoble, servile, inferior.
Nobody	x	Somebody, celebrity, eminence.

Nocturnal	x	Daily, diurnal, light.
Noise	x	Calm, quiet, tranquility.
Noiseless	x	Noisy, clamorous, boisterous.
Noisome	x	Inoffensive, aromatic, moral.
Noisy	x	Noiseless, calm, muted.
Nominal	x	Actual, real, consequential.
Nominate	x	Condemn, depose, cancel.
Nonentity	x	Entity, celebrity, somebody.
Nonsense	x	Sense, judgment, wisdom.
Normal	x	Abnormal, exceptional, peculiar.
Notable	x	Ordinary, average, insignificant.
Note	x	Ignore, discredit, disregard.
Nothing	x	Something, anyhow, exactly.
Notice	x	Disdain, disregard, neglect.
Notify	x	Withhold, conceal, refrain.
Notion	x	Misconception, actuality, reality.
Notorious	x	Famous, reputed, anonymous.
Nourish	x	Famish, abandon, harm.

Nourishment	x	Candy, deprivation, starvation.
Novel	x	Ancient, conventional, common.
Novice	x	Veteran, expert, professional.
Now	x	Then, eventually, later,
Nowhere	x	Everywhere, abnormal, extraordinary.
Noxious	x	Beneficial, harmless, healthful.
Nucleus	x	Exterior, face, periphery.
Nude	x	Covered, clothed, decent.
Nudity	x	Clothing, dress, vestment.
Nugatory	x	Legal, adequate, beneficial.
Nuisance	x	Entertainment, pleasure, comfort.
Null	x	Valid, legal, worthy.
Nullify	x	Allow, approve, enact.
Numb	x	Alive, sensitive, expressive.
Number	x	Guess, conjecture, mass.
Numberless	x	Numbered, finite, limited.
Numerous	x	Few, limited, unimportant.
Nuptial	x	Non-marital, divorce, separate.

Nurse	x	Neglect, starve, destroy.
Nurture	x	Neglect, deprive, hinder.
Nutriment	x	Starvation, exhaustion, deprivation.

O

Oath	x	Fulfillment, blessing, break.
Obdurate	x	Tender, yielding, obedient.
Obedience	x	Disobedience, breach, disregard.
Obedient	x	Disobedient, defiant, arrogant.
Obesity	x	Leanness, fitness, thinness.
Obey	x	Disobey, resist, refuse.
Object	x	Consent, subject, nonentity.
Object	x	Subject, nonentity, method.
Objective	x	Subjective, biased, involved.
Obligation	x	Choice, asset, irresponsibility.
Oblige	x	Disoblige, allow, release.
Obliging	x	Disobliging, arrogant, unfriendly.
Oblique	x	Balanced, parallel, straightforward.

Oblivion	x	Memory, recollection, caring.
Obloquy	x	Praise, approval, esteem,
Obnoxious	x	Pleasant, acceptable, appealing.
Obscure	x	Clear, definite, bright.
Obsequious	x	Sincere, assertive, arrogant.
Observance	x	Inobservance, breach, disregard.
Observant	x	Unobservant, absent, careless.
Observation	x	Inobservance, ignorance, disregard.
Observe	x	Overlook, defy, break.
Obsolete	x	Current, active, contemporary.
Obstacle	x	Advantage, catalyst, assistance.
Obstinacy	x	Irresolution, broadmindedness, docility.
Obstinate	x	Amenable, obedient, docile.
Obstruct	x	Aid, accelerate, promote.
Obstruction	x	Aid, assistance, advantage.
Obtain	x	Lose, forfeit, disperse.
Obtainable	x	Unobtainable, unavailable, unachievable.
Obtrude	x	Void, shun, disregard.

Obtuse	x	Acute, apt, bright.
Obverse	x	Synonym, copy, back.
Obvious	x	Obscure, ambiguous, concealed.
Occasionally	x	Frequently, always, commonly.
Occult	x	Obvious, clear, unequivocal.
Occupancy	x	Dispossession, vacancy, ejection.
Occupation	x	Avocation, hobby, ejection.
Occupy	x	Vacate, abandon, annoy.
Occur	x	Hide, lose, proceed.
Occurrence	x	Denial, reality, refusal.
Odd	x	Even, matched, similar.
Odious	x	Innocuous, pleasing, acceptable.
Odium	x	Admiration, affection, esteem.
Odorous	x	Inodorous, odorless, scentless.
Offence	x	Defense, protection, innocence.
Offend	x	Please, sooth, forgive.
Offensive	x	Defensive, inoffensive, acceptable.
Offer	x	Refuse, denial, idleness.

Offhand	x	Premeditated, careful, deliberate.
Office	x	Alternative, unemployment, postponement.
Officer	x	Civilian, employee, member.
Official	x	Unofficial, imprecise, non-official.
Officiate	x	Cease, follow, neglect.
Officious	x	Modest, quiet, unobtrusive.
Often	x	Seldom, infrequently, never.
Old	x	Young, new, fresh.
Older	x	Younger, adolescent, immature.
Ominous	x	Auspicious, bright, pleasant.
Omit	x	Add, consider, regard.
Omnipotent	x	Impotent, inefficient, helpless.
Omniscient	x	Foolish, unknowing, ignorant.
On	x	Off, broken, inactive.
One	x	Diverse, manifold, several, few.
Onerous	x	Effortless, easy, calm.
Only	x	Divers, myriad, collectively.
Onset	x	Cessation, defense, conclusion.

Onward	x	Backward, rearward, back.
Opaque	x	Transparent, pellucid, intelligible.
Open	x	Close, restricted, biased.
Opening	x	Closing, obstruction, termination.
Operation	x	Disuse, exertion, cessation.
Opinion	x	Fact, denial, evidence.
Opponent	x	Ally, friend, accomplice.
Opportune	x	Inopportune, untimely, abrupt.
Opportunity	x	Close, misfortune, adversity.
Oppose	x	Support, accept, abide.
Opposite	x	Alike, synonymous, non-contradictory.
Opposition	x	Acceptance, accord, correlation.
Oppress	x	Encourage, comfort, aid.
Oppression	x	Kindness, bliss, help.
Oppressive	x	Comfortable, luxurious, compassionate.
Opprobrium	x	Popularity, credit, elevation.
Option	x	Necessity, compulsion, coercion.
Optional	x	Compulsory, mandatory, obligatory.

Opulence	x	Poverty debt, dearth.
Oracular	x	Unambiguous, un-prophetic, cautious.
Oral	x	Written, explicit, printed.
Oration	x	Silence, hush, silence.
Oratory	x	Hesitation, stammering, dullness.
Orbit	x	Inside, interior, deviation.
Ordain	x	Cancel, repeal, revoke.
Ordeal	x	Comfort, contentment, happiness.
Order	x	Disorder, disorganization, confusion.
Orderly	x	Disorderly, chaotic, confused.
Ordinary	x	Extraordinary, different, unusual.
Organic	x	Inorganic, Non-essential, secondary.
Organization	x	Disorganization, imbalance, disproportion.
Organize	x	Disorganize, mess, derange.
Origin	x	End, conclusion, extinction.
Original	x	Duplicate, advanced, imitative.
Originate	x	Cease, conclude, perish.
Ornament	x	Blemish, blot, disgrace.

Ornate	x	Bare, prosaic, dull.
Orthodox	x	Unorthodox, unconventional, radical.
Ostensible	x	Genuine, improbable, actual.
Ostentation	x	Concealment, austerity, modesty.
Ostracism	x	Acceptance, allowance, welcome.
Oust	x	Retain, accept, welcome.
Out	x	In, here, existing.
Outbreak	x	Calm, doldrums, peace.
Outcry	x	Mumble, quiet, acceptance.
Outer	x	Inner, interior, center.
Outlet	x	Entrance, access, closure.
Outline	x	Inside, amplification, expansion.
Outrage	x	Advantage, delight, pleasure.
Outrageous	x	Inoffensive, moderate, gentle.
Outside	x	Inside, inner, great.
Outskirts	x	Downtown, interior, midtown.
Outstanding	x	Common, inferior, average.
Outward	x	Inward, inner, obscure.

Over	x	Under, incomplete, undone.
Overcast	x	Bright, luminous, cloudless.
Overcome	x	Lose, collapse, indifferent.
Overflow	x	Dearth, deficiency, trickle.
Overpower	x	Yield, defeat, upset.
Overruling	x	Allow, approve, support.
Oversight	x	Accuracy, precision, success.
Overt	x	Covert, obscure, uncertain.
Overthrow	x	Establish, restore, success.
Overture	x	Acceptance, refusal, conclusion.
Overweening	x	Modest, unassuming, deficient.
Overwhelm	x	Admit, confess, encourage.
Owe	x	Repay, resolve, settle.
Own	x	Disown, abandon, lose.
Owner	x	Hirer, renter, tenant.

P

Pacific	x	Turbulent, agitated, aggressive.
Pacification	x	Surrender, arming, build up.
Pacify	x	Infuriate, annoy, discharge.
Pack	x	Unpack, excavate, scoop.
Pact	x	Discord, disagreement, disagreement.
Paean	x	Censure, correction, admonition.
Pagan	x	Christian, believer, religious.
Paganism	x	Belief, trust, agreement.
Pageant	x	Hiding, illusion, reality.
Paid	x	Unpaid, dismiss, fire.
Pain	x	Pleasure, comfort, solace.
Painful	x	Painless, agreeable, pleasant.
Painstaking	x	Careless, apathetic, neglectful.

Paint	x	Reveal, uncover, whiten.
Pair	x	One, single, disconnect.
Palatable	x	Unpalatable, disagreeable, unacceptable.
Pale	x	Bright, clear, definite.
Palliate	x	Aggravate, accuse, harm.
Palm	x	Collapse, defeat, overlook.
Palpable	x	Impalpable, abstract, intangible.
Paltry	x	Admirable, big, considerable.
Panegyric	x	Censure, correction, abuse.
Pang	x	Comfort, happiness, ease.
Parable	x	History, fact, narrative.
Parade	x	Concealment, hiding, dullness.
Paradise	x	Hell, misery, depression.
Paradox	x	Normality, standard, answer.
Parallel	x	Different, variable, crooked.
Paralyze	x	Nerve, strengthen, build.
Paramount	x	Lowest, inferior, last.
Parasite	x	Benefactor, supporter, blessing.

Pardon	x	Penalty, conviction, accuse.
Pardonable	x	Unpardonable, inexcusable, defendable.
Parity	x	Disparity, difference, discrepancy.
Parsimonious	x	Generous, bountiful, selfless.
Part	x	Whole, altogether, absolutely.
Partake	x	Abstain, fast, forfeit.
Partial	x	Impartial, complete, universal.
Partially	x	Impartially, absolutely, totally.
Particle	x	Abundance, mass, lot.
Particular	x	General, ambiguous, concise.
Parting	x	Beginning, union, meeting.
Partisan	x	Unbiased, impartial, fair.
Partition	x	Unification, union, aid.
Partly	x	Fully, completely, plain.
Partly	x	Wholly, altogether, completely.
Partner	x	Competitor, opponent, adversary, bachelor.
Partnership	x	Separation, disaffiliation, division.
Pass	x	Fail, denial, refusal.

Passable	x	Impassable, nonporous, inadequate.
Passion	x	Indifference, apathy, frigidity.
Passive	x	Active, caring, resistant.
Past	x	Future, present, current.
Pastime	x	Work, fatigue, profession.
Patent	x	Ambiguous, concealed, dubious.
Paternal	x	Maternal, motherly, filial.
Pathetic	x	Cheering, admirable, decent.
Pathless	x	Passable, accessible, crowded.
Patience	x	Impatience, defiance, agitation.
Patient	x	Impatient, bored, fed up.
Patrician	x	Common, inferior, illegitimate.
Patriotic	x	Unpatriotic, traitorous, treasonous.
Pattern	x	Disorder, plainness, confusion.
Paucity	x	Abundance, sufficiency, bountiful.
Pause	x	Proceed, continuation, start.
Pay	x	Default, debt, penalty.
Payment	x	Nonpayment, non-remittal, underpayment.

Peace	x	War, conflict, agitation.
Peaceable	x	Violent, unfriendly, hostile.
Peculiar	x	Unusual, common, nonspecific.
Peculiarity	x	Simplicity, conformity, sameness.
Pedigree	x	Issue, progeny, seed.
Peer	x	Superior, inferior, opponent.
Peerless	x	Imperfect, mediocre, common.
Peevish	x	Congenial, affable, friendly.
Penal	x	Non-punitive, compensatory, remitting.
Penalty	x	Reward, amnesty, gain.
Pendent	x	Certain, clear, definite.
Penetrate	x	Depart, leave, surrender.
Penetration	x	Departure, egress, evacuation.
Penitence	x	Impenitence, approval, comfort.
Penitent	x	Impenitent, pitiless, unrepentant.
Penniless	x	Rich, affluent, comfortable.
Pensive	x	Unreflective, joyous, thoughtless.
Penurious	x	Affluent, liberal, bountiful.

Penury	x	Prosperity, abundance, luxury.
Perceivable	x	Imperceptible, ignore, miss.
Perceive	x	Ignore, lose, miss.
Perception	x	Conception, ignorance, stupidity.
Percolate	x	Flood, gush, pour.
Perdition	x	Exoneration, bliss, glory.
Peremptory	x	Humble, chosen, elective.
Perennial	x	Ceasing, occasional, intermittent.
Perfect	x	Imperfect, deficient, corrupt.
Perfectly	x	Imperfectly, faultily, inaccurately.
Perfidious	x	Dutiful, dedicated, constant.
Perform	x	Abstain, fail, ignore.
Performance	x	Nonperformance, failure, omission.
Perfume	x	Stench, odor, stink.
Perfunctory	x	Attentive, concerned, careful.
Perhaps	x	Improbably, never, unlikely.
Peril	x	Safety, protection, certainty.
Period	x	Eternity, beginning, genesis.

Periodical	x	Aperiodic, episodic, eternal.
Permanent	x	Impermanent, temporary, ephemeral.
Permission	x	Denial, refusal, ban.
Permit	x	Prohibit, ban, deter.
Pernicious	x	Advantageous, beneficial, healthful.
Perpetual	x	Impermanent, discontinuous, momentary.
Perplex	x	Simplify, enlighten, abbreviate.
Perplexity	x	Assurance, harmony, certainty.
Perseverance	x	Apathy, indifference, instability.
Persist	x	Perish, quit, surrender.
Personal	x	Impersonal, popular, shared.
Perspicacity	x	Dullness, bluntness, insensibility.
Perspicuity	x	Ambiguity, obscurity, imprecision.
Persuade	x	Dissuade, discourage, deter.
Pertinent	x	Impertinent, extraneous, improper.
Pertness	x	Care, bashfulness, humility.
Perverse	x	Compliant, affable, pure.
Petition	x	Claim, protest, demand.

Petty	x	Important, greater, considerable.
Petulant	x	Polite, affable, cordial.
Philanthropy	x	Greediness, selfishness, barbarity.
Philosophical	x	Non-philosophical, irrational, emotional.
Physical	x	Immaterial, mental, spiritual.
Pick	x	Put, reject, force.
Picturesque	x	Ambiguous, awkward, ugly.
Piece	x	Whole, aggregate, compound.
Piety	x	Impiety, atheism, hypocrisy.
Pinnacle	x	Base, bottom, nadir.
Pioneer	x	Follower, consequent, advanced.
Pious	x	Impious, irreligious, atheist.
Piquant	x	Flat, dull, insipid.
Pique	x	Delight, approval, satisfaction.
Piteous	x	Joyous, comfortable, august.
Pitiable	x	Enviable, decent, respectable.
Pitiful	x	Cheerful, admirable, decent.
Pity	x	Cruelty, mercilessness, brutality.

Place	x	Displace, benefit, misplace.
Placid	x	Agitated, anxious, distracted, crazy.
Plain	x	Complicated, adorned, artful.
Planned	x	Accidental, unplanned, casual.
Plant	x	Eradicate, uproot, animal.
Plausible	x	Implausible, absurd, incredible.
Play	x	Work, gravity, earnest.
Plead	x	Protest, answer, grant.
Pleasant	x	Unpleasant, agitated, gloomy.
Please	x	Displease, anger, aggravate.
Pleasure	x	Sorrow, misery, bore.
Plenitude	x	Want, scarcity, scantiness.
Plentiful	x	Scarce, deficient, scant.
Plight	x	Advantage, solution, blessing.
Plot	x	Ignorance, innocence, decrease.
Poetical	x	Prosaic, literal, un-lyrical.
Poignant	x	Blunt, insipid, inexpressive.
Poisonous	x	Nonpoisonous, beneficial, nontoxic.

Polished	x	Unpolished, dim, barbaric.
Polite	x	Impolite, arrogant, thoughtless.
Politeness	x	Impoliteness, rudeness, audacity.
Polluted	x	Unpolluted, fine, pure.
Poor	x	Rich, affluent, lush.
Popular	x	Unpopular, unfashionable, exceptional.
Portion	x	Whole, entirely, sum.
Positive	x	Negative, denying, indefinite.
Possession	x	Dispossession, ejection, lack.
Possible	x	Impossible, unlikely, impractical.
Postpone	x	Expedite, advance, forward.
Potent	x	Impotent, delicate, week.
Potential	x	Actual, authentic, unlikely.
Poverty	x	Abundance, prosperity, riches.
Power	x	Powerless, impotence, feebleness.
Practicable	x	Impracticable, unrealistic, impossible.
Practice	x	Theory, abstention, neglect.
Praise	x	Curse, abuse, blame.

Precarious	x	Actual, certain, protected.
Precaution	x	Carelessness, imprudence, inattention.
Precede	x	Succeed, follow, postdate.
Precept	x	Ambiguity, answer, unbelief.
Precise	x	Inaccurate, ambiguous, approximate.
Precision	x	Vagueness, carelessness, inaccuracy.
Predatory	x	Protecting, gentle, herbivorous.
Predestination	x	Choice, free will, accident.
Prediction	x	Proof, reality, truth.
Preface	x	Conclusion, epilogue, conclusion.
Prefer	x	Decline, refuse, reject.
Prejudice	x	Impartiality, neutrality, reason.
Preliminary	x	Final, subsequent, following.
Premature	x	Mature, belated, expected
Premium	x	Cheap, inexpensive, penalty.
Prenatal	x	Postnatal, perinatal, postpartum.
Prepared	x	Unprepared, extempore, unfixed.
Preposterous	x	Reasonable, realistic, brainy.

Presence	x	Absence, distance, separation.
Present	x	Past, absent, future.
Preservation	x	Damage, danger, neglect.
Presumption	x	Modesty, fact, bashfulness.
Pretend	x	Authentic, convincing, genuine.
Pretending	x	Unpretending, genuine, natural.
Pretense	x	Reality, honesty, simplicity.
Pretty	x	Ugly, unpleasant, unattractive.
Prevalence	x	Infrequence, uncommonness, rareness.
Previous	x	Later, after, advanced.
Pride	x	Humility, modesty, depression.
Primary	x	Secondary, subsequent, inferior.
Prime	x	Ancillary, awful, base.
Primeval	x	Advanced, complex, modern.
Principal	x	Subordinate, ancillary, inessential.
Principle	x	Ambiguity, effect, result.
Principled	x	Unprincipled, immoral, dishonest.
Prior	x	Later, prior, future.

Private	x	Public, common, open.
Prize	x	Atrocious, loss, inferior.
Probable	x	Improbable, absurd, doubtful.
Proceed	x	Recede, remain, retreat.
Proclaim	x	Conceal, silence, recall.
Proclaimed	x	Unproclaimed, conceal, suppress.
Prodigal	x	Frugal, economical, conserving.
Produce	x	Destroy, impede, restrict.
Productive	x	Unproductive, barren, impotent.
Profession	x	Avocation, hobby, denial.
Professional	x	Amateur, inexperienced, inefficient.
Proficient	x	Unskilled, amateur, incapable.
Profit	x	Loss, damage, charge.
Profitable	x	Unprofitable, fruitless, damaging.
Profound	x	Superficial, shallow, simple.
Profuse	x	Scarce, bare, minimal.
Progress	x	Regress, backwash, decrease.
Progressive	x	Reactionary, conventional, orthodox.

Prohibit	x	Permit, allow, approve.
Prolific	x	Barren, infertile, meager.
Prolix	x	Compact, precise, short.
Prologue	x	Epilogue, conclusion, ending.
Prominent	x	Inconspicuous, subtle, anonymous.
Promote	x	Demote, degrade, block.
Prompt	x	Delinquent, behind, unresponsive.
Pronounce	x	Mispronounce, mumble, conceal.
Propagate	x	Suppress, restrict, decrease.
Proper	x	Improper, defective, causal.
Properly	x	Improperly, incorrectly, unseemly.
Propitiation	x	Alienation, condemnation, curse.
Propitious	x	Inauspicious, unfortunate, dim.
Proportion	x	Disproportion, disparity, entirety.
Proposal	x	Acceptance, denial, condemnation.
Proposition	x	Reality, acceptance, certainty.
Propriety	x	Impropriety, indecency, crudeness.
Prosperity	x	Adversity, decrease, poverty.

Prosperity	x	Poverty, misfortune, misery.
Protect	x	Expose, endanger, abandon.
Protest	x	Support, agreement, peace.
Protract	x	Contract, abbreviate, reduce.
Proud	x	Humble, modest, egoless.
Prove	x	Disprove, refute, challenge.
Provide	x	Conserve, neglect, withhold.
Provided	x	Unprovided, conserve, withhold.
Provisional	x	Permanent, final, extended.
Provocation	x	Subduing, compliment, respect.
Provoke	x	Placate, appease, bridle.
Provoked	x	Unprovoked, calm, pacify.
Prowess	x	Cowardice, failure, timidity.
Prudence	x	Imprudence, indiscretion, rashness.
Prudent	x	Imprudent, reckless, unwise.
Public	x	Private, classified, confidential.
Publish	x	Suppress, censure, conceal.
Punctilious	x	Casual, impolite, improper.

Punctual	x	Tardy, belated, behind.
Pungent	x	Pleasant, aged, ripe.
Punish	x	Reward, excuse, spare.
Puny	x	Big, important, grant.
Pupil	x	Non-student, expert, teacher.
Purchase	x	Sell, exchange, deal.
Pure	x	Impure, adulterated, obscene.
Purity	x	Impurity, immodesty, sinfulness.
Purpose	x	Aimlessness, chance, hatred.
Purposeful	x	Purposeless, irresolute, unintentional.
Push	x	Pull, hesitation, idleness.
Put	x	Take, remove, displace.
Putrefy	x	Flourish, combine, develop.
Putrid	x	Fresh, sweet, incorrupt.
Puzzling	x	Lucid, clear, explicit.

Quack	x	Savant, expert, genuine.
Quaint	x	Modest, average, common.
Quake	x	Stiffen, face, fix.
Qualification	x	Disqualification, ignorance, inability.
Qualified	x	Unqualified, incompetent, unfit.
Quality	x	Dis quality, atrocious, inferior.
Qualm	x	Composed, confidence, certainty.
Quandary	x	Calm, solution, breeze.
Quantity	x	Bit, insignificance, atom.
Quarrel	x	Amity, accord, harmony.
Quarrelsome	x	Peaceful, nonaggressive, un combatable.
Quash	x	Uphold, encourage, abet.
Queer	x	Normal, common, customary.

Quell	x	Incite, agitate, stir.
Querulous	x	Cheerful, affable, easy.
Query	x	Answer, response, agreement.
Quest	x	Response, relinquish, surrender.
Question	x	Answer, reply, respond.
Questionable	x	Unquestionable, certain, definite.
Quick	x	Slow, unresponsive, clumsy.
Quicken	x	Decelerate, hinder, dampen.
Quickly	x	Slowly, eventually, later.
Quickness	x	Slowness, sluggishness, procrastination.
Quiet	x	Noisy, action, agitation.
Quote	x	Misquote, insert, omit.

R

Rabble	x	Aristocracy, nobility, elite.
Rabid	x	Mild, moderate, delighted.
Racy	x	Dull, apathetic, boring.
Radiant	x	Dull, lusterless, gloomy.
Radical	x	Orthodox, conservative, impartial.
Rage	x	Placidity, calmness, patience.
Rainy	x	Rainless, dry, hot.
Raise	x	Lower, decrease, degrade.
Ramble	x	Speed, run, proceed.
Random	x	Methodical, systematic, arranged.
Ransom	x	Confine, harm, forfeit.
Rapid	x	Slow, delayed, crowing.
Rapidity	x	Slowness, delay, retardation.

Rare	x	Common, frequent, abundant.
Rarely	x	Commonly, frequently, regularly.
Rash	x	Cautious, deliberate, careful.
Rational	x	Irrational, absurd, illogical.
Raw	x	Ripe, cooked, refined.
Reach	x	Depart, abandon, go away.
Reactionary	x	Revolutionary, liberal, modernist.
Ready	x	Unready, abstruse, unskilled.
Real	x	Unreal, artificial, counterfeit.
Realism	x	Nominalism, inaccuracy, unreality.
Realistic	x	Unrealistic, idealistic, impractical.
Reality	x	Unreality, fantasy, inexistence.
Reap	x	Sow, plant grow.
Rear	x	Anterior, front, forward.
Reason	x	Delusion, illogic, unreason.
Reasoning	x	Unreasoning, irrationality, illogical.
Reassure	x	Discourage, distress, demoralize.
Rebellious	x	Loyal, amenable, obedient

Rebuke	x	Praise, acclamation, endorsement.
Recall	x	Forget, misremember, ignore.
Recant	x	Accept, admit, adopt.
Recede	x	Advance, emerge, accumulate.
Recent	x	Ancient, before, future.
Reception	x	Expulsion, rejection, denial.
Recite	x	Read, generalize, misquote.
Reckless	x	Cautious, careful, responsible.
Recognize	x	Deny, discredit, ignore.
Reconcile	x	Separate, alienate, estrange.
Reconciliation	x	Separation, estrangement, alienation.
Recorded	x	Unrecorded, unregistered, untapped.
Recover	x	Lose, ail, sicken.
Recoverable	x	Irrecoverable, decline, ail.
Recovery	x	Loss, decline, deterioration.
Recreation	x	Bore, drag, fatigue.
Rectitude	x	Corruption, dishonesty, immorality.
Redden	x	Pale, whiten, lighten.

Redemption	x	Captivity, confinement, desertion.
Reduce	x	Increase, add, amplify.
Redundant	x	Deficient, inadequate, scarce.
Refinement	x	Coarseness, corruption, brutality.
Reflect	x	Conceal, hide, withhold.
Reform	x	Damage, deform, impair.
Refuge	x	Closure, exposure, danger.
Refusal	x	Acceptance, approval, sanction.
Refuse	x	Accept, refuse, approve.
Refute	x	Support, accept, adopt.
Regard	x	Disregard, neglect, condemnation.
Regress	x	Progress, develop, forge.
Regret	x	Calmness, joy, remorselessness.
Regular	x	Irregular, abnormal, infrequent.
Regulation	x	Deregulation, disorder, anarchy.
Rehearse	x	Neglect, generalize, forget.
Reject	x	Accept, admit, grant.
Rejoice	x	Grieve, mourn, regret.

Related	x	Unrelated, different, distinct.
Relation	x	Non-relative, break up, separation.
Relative	x	Absolute, genuine, complete.
Relax	x	Tighten, agitate, strain.
Release	x	Arrest, imprisonment, condemn.
Relevant	x	Irrelevant, improper, frivolous.
Reliable	x	Unreliable, uncertain, disloyal.
Relief	x	Discomfort, oppression, unhappiness.
Religion	x	Irreligion, atheism, agnosticism.
Religious	x	Secular, nonreligious, worldly.
Relinquish	x	Retain, allow, keep.
Reluctant	x	Willing, eager, disposed.
Remain	x	Leave, abscond, cease.
Remarkable	x	Unremarkable, average, general.
Remember	x	Forget, disremember, disregard.
Remembrance	x	Oblivion, forgetfulness, amnesia.
Reminiscence	x	Oblivion, forgetfulness, announcement.
Remitter	x	Recipient, appear, emerge.

Remote	x	Near, distinct, exposed.
Removable	x	Irremovable, tenured, ineradicable.
Remove	x	Place, accept, wear.
Rend	x	Mend, attach, agree.
Render	x	Keep, retain, refuse.
Renounce	x	Preserve, acknowledge, embrace.
Renown	x	Anonymity, disgrace, obscurity.
Renowned	x	Notorious, anonymous, obscure.
Renunciation	x	Acceptance, indulgence, embrace.
Repair	x	Disrepair, damage, disorder.
Repeat	x	Discontinue, original, interrupt.
Repel	x	Attract, accept, agree.
Repentance	x	Impenitence, remorselessness, happiness.
Repenting	x	Unrepenting, delight, relish.
Repletion	x	Scarcity, lack, insufficiency.
Reply	x	Question, action, challenge.
Report	x	Discredit, conceal, ignorance.
Repose	x	Agitation, bustle, action.

Represent	x	Misrepresent, refuse, oppose.
Reprimand	x	Compliment, condemnation, citation.
Reproach	x	Approval, acclamation, credit.
Reproof	x	Commendation, approval, praise.
Reprove	x	Approve, abet, endorse.
Repudiate	x	Affirm, accept, approve.
Repugnant	x	Acceptable, inoffensive, amicable.
Reputable	x	Disreputable, discreditable, ordinary.
Repute	x	Disgrace, discredit, dishonour.
Required	x	Unrequired, optional, voluntary.
Requite	x	Absolve, forgive, owe.
Research	x	Ignorance, ignore, inobservance.
Resemblance	x	Difference, divergence, dissimilarity.
Reserve	x	Abandonment, archetype, emptiness.
Reserved	x	Unreserved, agitated, troubled.
Reside	x	Vacate, depart, leave.
Resident	x	Visitor, foreigner, transient.
Resign	x	Remain, assert, claim.

Resignation	x	Resistance, stay, arrogance.
Resist	x	Tolerate, accept, capitulate.
Resistance	x	Surrender, acceptance, obedience.
Resistible	x	Irresistible, resistless, overpowering.
Resolute	x	Irresolute, undetermined, docile.
Resources	x	Debt, liabilities, poverty.
Respect	x	Contempt, disapproval, disfavour.
Respectable	x	Unworthy, dishonest, disreputable.
Respective	x	Irrespective, indefinite, identical.
Resplendent	x	Dull, ugly, dark.
Respond	x	Ignore, request, ask.
Responsible	x	Irresponsible, innocent, exempt.
Rest	x	Unrest, agitation, action.
Restive	x	Restful, gentle, obedient.
Restore	x	Remove, take, damage.
Restrain	x	Liberate, loose, discharge.
Restrained	x	Unrestrained, graceless, flaring.
Result	x	Cause, beginning, antecedent.

Retail	x	Wholesale, buy, purchase.
Retain	x	Relinquish, abandon, exclude.
Retard	x	Quicken, propel, accelerate.
Retirement	x	Advance, company, association.
Retribution	x	Clemency, forgiveness, compassion.
Retrospect	x	Prospect, forethought, preview.
Return	x	Depart, charge, challenge.
Reveal	x	Conceal, contradict, deny.
Revelation	x	Concealment, cover up, secret.
Revenge	x	Pardon, clemency, forgiveness.
Revenue	x	Expense, charge, debt.
Reverse	x	Front, stagnation, duplicate.
Revert	x	Promote, grow, develop.
Revive	x	Extinguish, restart, faint.
Revoke	x	Enforce, continue, affirm.
Revolution	x	Counterrevolution, harmony, order.
Revolve	x	Bind, disregard, grind.
Reward	x	Punishment, acquit, disgrace.

Rich	x	Poor, destitute, meager.
Riches	x	Poverty, debt, liabilities.
Riddle	x	Solution, axiom, answer.
Ridicule	x	Admiration, applause, approval.
Right	x	Wrong, bogus, artificial.
Righteous	x	Corrupt, improper, unprincipled.
Rigid	x	Flexible, indefinite, broken.
Ripe	x	Raw, unripe, immature.
Rise	x	Fall, descend, decline.
Risky	x	Safe, harmless, certain.
Rival	x	Friend, accomplice, partner.
Rivalry	x	Friendship, concord, harmony.
Roar	x	Whisper, murmur, quiet.
Robust	x	Feeble, delicate, impotent.
Roll	x	Unroll, unwind, stagnation.
Romantic	x	Unromantic, unsentimental, pragmatic.
Root	x	Uproot, effect, result.
Rough	x	Smooth, nonviolent, gentle.

Roughness	x	Smoothness, courtesy, mildness.
Round	x	Flat, straight, lean.
Royal	x	Beggarly, ignoble, humble.
Rude	x	Polite, refined, cultured.
Rugged	x	Smooth, even, easy.
Rule	x	Misrule, lawlessness, exception.
Run	x	Walk, malfunction, stop.
Rupture	x	Union, agreement, attach.
Rural	x	Urban, cultured, metropolitan.
Rush	x	Tarry, stay, reluctant.
Rustic	x	Sophisticated, elegant, serene.
Rustle	x	Inertness, crawl, delay.
Ruthless	x	Merciful, benevolent, civilized.

S

Sable	x	White, bright, cheerful.
Sacred	x	Profane, earthly, bad.
Sacrifice	x	Gain, refuse, offense.
Sad	x	Cheerful, joyous, presentable.
Safe	x	Risky, damaged, harmed.
Safeguard	x	Endanger, harm, injure.
Safety	x	Danger, distress, peril.
Sagacious	x	Silly, absurd, careless.
Sage	x	Idiot, dense, dull.
Saint	x	Sinner, backslider, beast.
Salient	x	Common, unimportant, unnoticeable.
Salutary	x	Pernicious, damaging, unfriendly.
Salvation	x	Damnation, destruction, decimation.

Same   x   Different, dissimilar, unequal.

Sample   x   Whole, aggregate, abnormality.

Sanction   x   Prohibition, disapproval, cancellation.

Sane   x   Insane, foolish, unbalanced.

Sanguine   x   Hesitant, depressed, doubtful.

Sanitary   x   Insanitary, unhygienic, unsterile.

Sanity   x   Insanity, mania, delusion.

Sarcasm   x   Compliment, acclaim, praise.

Satanic   x   Devine, celestial, heavenly.

Satire   x   Eulogy, seriousness, respectful.

Satisfaction   x   Dissatisfaction, misery, discontent.

Satisfy   x   Dissatisfy, deprive, irritate.

Saucy   x   Meek, respectful, kind.

Savage   x   Civilized, cultured, gentle.

Save   x   Endanger, waste, neglect.

Say   x   Hear, silence, listen.

Scarce   x   Plenty, abundant, common.

Scarcity   x   Abundance, excess, sufficiency.

Scathing	x	Gentle, amusing, calm.
Scatter	x	Gather, collect, crowd.
Scheme	x	Disorder, honesty, causality.
Scholar	x	Fool, nonstudent, ignorant.
Scholarly	x	Unscholarly, illiterate, uneducated.
Science	x	Nescience, ignorance, fallacy.
Scientific	x	Unscientific, pseudoscientific, artistic.
Scoff	x	Praise, nibble, approve.
Scorn	x	Respect, praise, acceptance.
Scoundrel	x	Gentleman, innocent, angel.
Screw	x	Unscrew, untwist, straiten.
Scruple	x	Calmness, contentment, abundance.
Scrupulous	x	Unscrupulous, careless, inaccurate, reckless.
Scrutiny	x	Flash, slight, inattention.
Sea	x	Land, air, lack.
Seal	x	Open, unseal, denial.
Season	x	Decondition, soften, sensitize.
Seasonable	x	Unseasonable, inopportune, untimely.

Secondary	x	Primary, fundamental, important.
Secret	x	Public, open, acknowledged.
Secure	x	Insecure, uncertain, dangerous.
Sedate	x	Agitated, disturbed, excited.
Sedition	x	Obedience, pacification, orderliness.
See	x	Ignore, miss, overlook.
Seek	x	Shun, find, ignore.
Seemly	x	Unbecoming, inappropriate, improper.
Seen	x	Unseen, disregard, forget.
Seize	x	Restore, free, misconceive.
Seldom	x	Often, frequently, generally.
Select	x	Exclude, select, disapprove.
Selection	x	Rejection, coercion, exclusion.
Selfish	x	Unselfish, selfless, benevolent.
Sell	x	Buy, purchase, keep.
Send	x	Bring, receive, retain.
Sender	x	Receiver, acquire, accept.
Senior	x	Junior, minor, unimportant.

Sensation	x	Apathy, unconsciousness, physicality.
Sense	x	Nonsense, imprudence, illogic.
Sensibility	x	Insensibility, coldness, numbness.
Sensitive	x	Insensitive, easy, effortless.
Sensual	x	Sober, harsh, uncomfortable.
Sentiment	x	Insensitiveness, actuality, concrete.
Separate	x	Unite, combine, connect.
Separation	x	Union, association, unification.
Sequence	x	Interruption, confusion, disorder.
Serene	x	Confused, agitated, excited.
Serious	x	Unserious, trifling minor.
Servant	x	Master, head, boss.
Serve	x	Hinder, withhold, command.
Service	x	Disservice, hindrance, loss.
Servile	x	Masterful, arrogant, lordly.
Servitude	x	Liberty, mastery, freedom.
Set	x	Unfixed, unsettle, nonspecific.
Settle	x	Unsettle, depopulate, abort.

Sever	x	Unite, assemble, associate.
Several	x	Few, same, one.
Severe	x	Mild, lenient, easy.
Shade	x	Light, blaze, glare.
Shady	x	Honest, clear, exposed.
Shakable	x	Unshakable, calm, equanimity.
Shake	x	Fasten, steady, hold.
Shallow	x	Deep, raised, full.
Shame	x	Shamelessness, fame, honour.
Shameful	x	Shameless, decent, reputable.
Shape	x	Disorder, deformity, material.
Share	x	Whole, total, entirely.
Sharp	x	Blunt, dull, inactive.
Shaved	x	Unshaved, mend, cover.
Sheepish	x	Daring, bold, outgoing.
Shelter	x	Expose, endanger, evict.
Shine	x	Dim, aversion, blackness.
Short	x	Long, abundant, enduring.

Shove	x	Draw, discourage, hinder.
Show	x	Hide, conceal, artlessness.
Shrewd	x	Dull, innocent, blunt.
Shrink	x	Swell, accumulate, enlarge.
Shut	x	Open, start, expand.
Sick	x	Healthy, fit, uncorrupt.
Side	x	Center, chief, superior.
Sight	x	Blindness, reality, absence.
Significant	x	Insignificant, trivial, helpless.
Signify	x	Hide, conceal, withhold.
Silence	x	Noise, uproar, fame.
Silly	x	Serious, intelligent, responsible.
Similar	x	Dissimilar, different, unrelated.
Similarity	x	Dissimilarity, difference, inequality.
Simple	x	Complex, adorned, critical.
Simplify	x	Amplify, complicate, obscure.
Sin	x	Virtue, holiness, purity.
Sincere	x	Insincere, deceitful, dishonest.

Sinful	x	Sinless, moral, legitimate.
Single	x	Double, married, attached.
Singular	x	Diverse, common, frequent.
Sink	x	Rise, float, uplift.
Sit	x	Stand, move, straighten.
Situation	x	Avocation, jobless, dislodgment.
Skeptic	x	Believer, optimistic, chump.
Skilled	x	Unskilled, inept, incompetent.
Skillful	x	Unskilled, crude, awkward.
Sky	x	Earth, pit, underworld.
Slander	x	Acclaim, approval, compliment.
Slang	x	Standard, diction, language.
Slavery	x	Freedom, liberty, independence.
Slender	x	Thick, adequate, plentiful.
Slippery	x	Rough, secure, upright.
Slow	x	Fast, active speedy.
Small	x	Big, enormous, important.
Smart	x	Dull, clumsy, ignorant.

Smile	x	Frown, gloom, glower.
Smooth	x	Rough, clumsy, hard.
Sneer	x	Compliment, praise, admire.
Sober	x	Drunk, agitated, eccentric.
Social	x	Antisocial, unsocial, aloof.
Society	x	Solitude, separation, disintegration.
Soft	x	Hard, unyielding, mighty.
Softness	x	Hardness, firmness, fortitude.
Soiled	x	Unsoiled, clean pure.
Solace	x	Sorrow, discord, anguish.
Solemnity	x	Lightness, simplicity, superficiality.
Solid	x	Liquid, unstable, weak.
Solitude	x	Companionship, togetherness, crowd.
Solution	x	Problem, question, confusion.
Solved	x	Unsolved, unresolved, complicated.
Something	x	Nothing, extensively, greatly.
Soon	x	Later, belatedly, slowly.
Soothe	x	Rouse, excite, agitate.

Sordid	x	Clean, noble, virtuous,
Sorrow	x	Joy, gaiety, bliss.
Sorry	x	Glad, cheering, hopeful.
Sort	x	Mix, animal, beast.
Soul	x	Body, matter, flesh.
Sound	x	Silence, suppress, unhealthy.
Sovereign	x	Dependent, limited, inferior.
Space	x	Fullness, confinement, limitation.
Spare	x	Ample, abundant, plentiful.
Sparkling	x	Dull, gloomy, stupid.
Sparse	x	Dense, adequate, populous.
Speak	x	Be quite, suppress, conceal.
Special	x	Ordinary, general, universal.
Specific	x	Vague, nonspecific, indefinite.
Specious	x	Absurd, candid, forthright.
Speculation	x	Certainty, proof, truth.
Speech	x	Speechless, hush, silence.
Speedy	x	Slow, delayed, crawling.

Spend	x	Save, build, hoard.
Spirit	x	Substance, inactivity, non-intoxicant.
Spiritual	x	Unspiritual, carnal, irreligious.
Spite	x	Goodwill, devotion, passion.
Splendid	x	Poor, lowly, insignificant.
Spontaneous	x	Deliberate, planned, non-mechanical.
Spread	x	Collect, gather, close.
Spring	x	Settle, end, result.
Spurn	x	Welcome, accept, condone.
Stable	x	Unstable, wavering, insecure.
Stagnant	x	Moving, active, dynamic.
Stain	x	Stainless, disinfect, glorify.
Stale	x	Fresh, new, original.
Stamped	x	Unstamped, drift, hang.
Stand	x	Advance, sit, yield.
Standard	x	Nonstandard, abnormal, average.
Start	x	Finish, end, close.
Starve	x	Satiate, feed, content.

State	x	Deny, contradict, disprove.
Static	x	Dynamic, mobile, unfixed.
Station	x	Removal, unsettle, disorganize.
Stationary	x	Portable, flexible, active.
Stay	x	Continuation, abandon, proceed.
Steadfast	x	Unsteady, inconstant, disloyal.
Steady	x	Unsteady, irregular, episodic.
Steep	x	Gradual, deficient, low.
Sterile	x	Fertile, contaminated, fruitful.
Stiff	x	Flexible, elastic, amenable.
Still	x	Disturbed, noisy, rough.
Stimulate	x	Dissuade, block, dampen.
Stimulus	x	Deterrent, bock, hindrance.
Stingy	x	Generous, abundant, extravagant.
Stir	x	Rest, calm, stillness.
Stop	x	Start, continuation, progress.
Store	x	Distribute, discard, dump.
Storm	x	Calm, pacify, stillness.

Stormy	x	Serene, pacific, nonviolent.
Story	x	Fact, truth, non-fiction.
Stout	x	Lean, thin, delicate.
Straight	x	Crooked, indirectly, broken.
Strain	x	Rest, health, relaxation.
Strait	x	Broad, comfort, benefit.
Strange	x	Familiar, customary, ordinary.
Strength	x	Weakness, impotency, insecurity.
Strenuous	x	Facile, easy, achievable.
Stretched	x	Compact, firm, solid.
Strict	x	Lax, lenient, tolerant.
Strife	x	Peace, accord, agreement.
Strike	x	Fondle, defend, resist.
Strong	x	Weak, dilute, inactive.
Stronger	x	Weaker, delicate, broken.
Stubborn	x	Tractable, accepting, yielding.
Studious	x	Illiterate, unscholarly, ignorant.
Study	x	Ignore, idleness, indifference.

Stupid	x	Bright, judicious, intelligent.
Stupidity	x	Intelligence, brilliancy, cleverness.
Stylish	x	Coarse, dowdy, unfashionable.
Subject	x	Monarch, foreigner, stranger.
Subjective	x	Objective, general, typical.
Subjugate	x	Capitulate, discharge, liberate.
Sublime	x	Low, debased, unimpressive.
Submissive	x	Disobedient, arrogant, authoritarian.
Submit	x	Resist, endure, stand.
Substantial	x	Unsubstantial, immaterial, weak.
Subtle	x	Strong, robust, Frank, blunt.
Subtract	x	Add, annex, expand.
Subvert	x	Conserve, elevate, dignify.
Succeed	x	Precede, antecede, deteriorate.
Success	x	Failure, defeat, non-achievement.
Sudden	x	Gradual, expected, anticipated.
Suffer	x	Withstand, calm, resist.
Sufficient	x	Insufficient, inadequate, scanty.

Suitable	x	Unsuitable, incompetent, unfit.
Sullen	x	Cheerful, blithe, bright.
Sum	x	Part, aggregate, imperfection.
Summit	x	Base, bottom, abyss.
Sunrise	x	Sunset, darkness, evening.
Superb	x	Bad, meager, undignified.
Superficial	x	Penetrating, deep, profound.
Superfluous	x	Lacking, reasonable, inadequate.
Superior	x	Inferior, subordinate, mediocre.
Superiority	x	Inferiority, imperfection, incapacity.
Supernatural	x	Natural, common, earthly.
Supple	x	Brittle, rigid, compact.
Supplier	x	Consumer, enduring, preserving.
Support	x	Oppose, disapprove, demolish.
Suppose	x	Ascertain, conclude, disbelieve.
Suppress	x	Express, assist, encourage.
Sure	x	Unsure, doubtful, fallible.
Surplus	x	Deficit, inadequate, lack.

Surrender	x	Conquer, resist, retain.
Suspense	x	Certainty, resumption, continuance.
Suspicious	x	Trustful, decisive, certain.
Sustenance	x	Starvation, deprivation, candy.
Sweet	x	Bitter, unsavory, disagreeable.
Swell	x	Dwindle, bad, inferior.
Swift	x	Slow, crawling, lazy.
Symbolical	x	Non- symbolic, actual.Literal.
Symmetry	x	Asymmetry, disproportion, disparity.
Sympathetic	x	Unsympathetic, insensitive, heartless.
Sympathy	x	Cruelty, antipathy, hatred.
Synonymous	x	Antonymous, different, dissimilar.
Synthetic	x	Natural, genuine, real.
System	x	Disorder, confusion, fraction.
Systematic	x	Sporadic, unsystematic, chaotic.

T

Taboo	x	Permissible, acceptable, allowable.
Tacit	x	Express, apparent, explicit.
Taciturn	x	Loquacious, communicative, outspoken.
Tactful	x	Tactless, reckless, careless.
Tail	x	Head, front, beginning.
Take	x	Give, reject, abstain.
Talent	x	Inability, ignorance, incompetence.
Talkative	x	Reserved, uncommunicative, quiet.
Tall	x	Short, tiny, cheap.
Tame	x	Wild, untamed, savage.
Tangible	x	Intangible, abstract, conceptual.
Tardy	x	Swift, punctual, prompt.
Tart	x	Gentle, sweet, sociable.

Taste	x	Tasteless, distaste, aversion.
Tasteful	x	Distasteful, stale, rough.
Taunt	x	Compliment, praise, approve.
Teach	x	Learn, mislead, confuse.
Tear	x	Mend, reattach, closure.
Tearful	x	Joyous, cheerful, happy.
Tease	x	Please, defend, protect.
Tedious	x	Easy, interesting, exciting.
Temerity	x	Carefulness, bashfulness, timidity.
Tempest	x	Calmness, peace, harmony.
Temporal	x	Non-temporal, eternal, spiritual.
Temporary	x	Permanent, final, lasting.
Tenant	x	Landlord, proprietor, landowner.
Tendency	x	Aversion, dislike, apathy.
Tender	x	Hard, tough, mighty.
Tense	x	Relaxed, flexible, loose.
Tension	x	Comfort, consolation, release.
Tentative	x	Permanent, absolute, complete.

Termination	x	Existence, beginning, continuance.
Terrestrial	x	Celestial, cosmic, heavenly.
Terrible	x	Calming, insignificant, amusing.
Terrific	x	Pacific, pleasant, atrocious.
Terror	x	Coolness, calmness, confidence.
Terse	x	Lengthy, tedious, wordy.
Tested	x	Untested, undependable, unproven.
Testimony	x	Disproof, rebuttal, charge.
Thankful	x	Thankless, ungrateful, aggrieved.
That	x	This, merely, scantly.
Theism	x	Atheism, disbelief, unbelief.
Then	x	Now, present, future.
Theology	x	Anthropology, atheism, blasphemy.
Theory	x	Practice, fact, disbelief.
Thesis	x	Antithesis, assurance, certainty.
Thick	x	Thin, accurate, rare.
Think	x	Distrust, disbelief, doubt.
Thought	x	Thoughtlessness, actuality, certainty.

Thrall	x	Free, liberty, mastery.
Threat	x	Guard, protection, safety.
Thrifty	x	Generous, extravagant, wasteful.
Throng	x	Solitude, loneliness, dispersion.
Tidings	x	Misinformation, ignorance, silence.
Tidy	x	Untidy, unkempt, chaotic.
Tie	x	Untie, detach, part.
Tight	x	Loose, penetrable, insecure.
Timely	x	Untimely, improper, unseasonal.
Timid	x	Bold, brave, adventurous.
Tinged	x	Achromatic, whiten, bleach.
Tiny	x	Big, giant, enormous.
Tip	x	Base, bottom, nadir.
Tire	x	Refresh, activate, excite.
Together	x	Separately, successively, independently.
Told	x	Untold, suppress, mislead.
Tolerable	x	Intolerable, unbearable, inadequate.
Top	x	Bottom, lowest, inferior.

Torment	x	Comfort, pleasure, enjoyment.
Total	x	Partial, imperfect, divided.
Totally	x	Partially, incompletely, vaguely.
Touchable	x	Untouchable, intangible, formless.
Tough	x	Smooth, soft, easy.
Toxic	x	Non-toxic, harmless, beneficial.
Traceable	x	Untraceable, abundance, lump.
Tractable	x	Stubborn, intractable, resistant.
Trade	x	Avocation, inactivity, disagreement.
Tragedy	x	Comedy, accomplishment, benefit.
Tragic	x	Comic, blessed, fortunate.
Trained	x	Untrained, decondition, incapable.
Traitor	x	Patriot, loyalist, defender.
Tranquil	x	Disturbed, agitated, anxious.
Transact	x	Abandon, stop, refrain.
Transaction	x	Inactivity, neglect, disagreement.
Transgression	x	Innocence, guiltlessness, purity.
Transient	x	Permanent, enduring, immortal.

Transparent	x	Opaque, ambiguous, cloudy.
Trap	x	Release, blessing, honesty.
Travel	x	Settle, dwell, reside.
Travelled	x	Untraveled, shun, alienate,
Treachery	x	Loyalty, faithfulness, devotion.
Treasure	x	Disgrace, burden, trash.
Treaty	x	Antagonism, discord, neutrality
Tremendous	x	Insignificant, unappealing, little.
Trial	x	Accepted, tested, definite.
Trick	x	Honesty, conformity, exposure.
Tricky	x	Frank, effortless, simple.
Trifle	x	Treasure, lot, buckle.
Triumph	x	Defeat, failure, unhappiness.
Trivial	x	Important, major, big.
Trouble	x	Comfort, safeness, solution.
Troubled	x	Untroubled, calm, content.
Trust	x	Distrust, doubt, disbelief.
Truth	x	Lie, untruth, falsehood.

Try	x	Leave, quit, abstention.
Tumult	x	Quiet, calm, control.
Tuneful	x	Tuneless, disharmonious, discordant.
Turbulent	x	Calm, peaceful, nonviolent.
Turn	x	Fixity, failure, inability.
Turned	x	Unturned, hurdle, obstacle.
Tutor	x	Pupil, student, disciple.
Twist	x	Untwist, Straiten, conformity.
Type	x	Mistype, disarrange, abnormality.
Typical	x	Uncommon, unusual, infrequent.
Tyrannous	x	Benevolent, limited, restricted.

U

Ugliness   x   Loveliness, beauty, fair.

Ugly   x   Beautiful, attractive, aesthetic.

Ultimate   x   First, beginning, eminent, auxiliary.

Unanimity   x   Discord, disagreement, oppose.

Unanimous   x   Discordant, divided, split.

Uncouth   x   Couth, agile, refined.

Unctuous   x   Blunt, direct, genuine.

Under   x   Over, above, aloft.

Underhand   x   Open, honest, ethical.

Understand   x   Misunderstand, misinterpret, disregard.

Understanding   x   Misunderstanding, inconsiderate, ignorance.

Undertake   x   Refuse, abandon, decline.

Uniform	x	Non-uniform, heterogeneous, changing.
Union	x	Separation, disconnection, detachment.
Unique	x	Common, familiar, unexceptional.
Unison	x	Discord, conflict, denial.
Unit	x	Whole, fraction, entirety.
Unite	x	Divide, disconnect, dissociate.
Unity	x	Diversity, disunion, conflict.
Universal	x	Specific, limited, uncommon.
Unruly	x	Orderly, amenable, calm.
Up	x	Down, continuing, valid.
Upbraid	x	Approve, compliment, sanction.
Upgrade	x	Degrade, lower, demote.
Uphold	x	Withhold, refute, protest.
Upon	x	Under, beneath, below.
Upper	x	Lower, inferior, unimportant.
Upright	x	Dishonest, horizontal, corrupt.
Uproar	x	Calm, order, mumble.
Upward	x	Downward, descending, downwardly.

Urbane	x	Rude, discourteous, impolite.
Urge	x	Disgust, hinder, distaste.
Urgent	x	Non-urgent, unimportant, immaterial.
Use	x	Misuse, disuse, harm.
Useful	x	Useless, harmful, futile.
Usual	x	Unusual, exceptional, rare.
Usurp	x	Give, refuse, offer.
Utility	x	Inutility, disadvantage, worthlessness.
Utilization	x	Non-utilization, misuse, misapply.
Utilize	x	Waste, misuse, misapply.
Utmost	x	Innermost, least, minimal.
Utter	x	Imperfect, uncertain, least.
Utterly	x	Partially, imperfectly, incompletely.

V

Vacancy	x	Fullness, employment, completeness.
Vacant	x	Occupied, full engaged.
Vacate	x	Occupy, fill, employ.
Vacation	x	Work time, term, continuation.
Vacillate	x	Adhere, continue, persist.
Vacillation	x	Certainty, steadiness, eagerness.
Vacuity	x	Fullness, abundance, completeness.
Vagabond	x	Settled, immobile, worker.
Vagary	x	Actuality, purpose, fact.
Vagrant	x	Sedentary, immobile, settled.
Vague	x	Clear, apparent, definite.
Vain	x	Adequate, useful, humble.
Valediction	x	Accord, agreement, greeting.

Valiant	x	Timid, cowardly, diffident.
Valid	x	Invalid, fallacious, counterfeit.
Validate	x	Invalidate, contradict, refute.
Validity	x	Weakness, impotency, ineffectiveness.
Valor	x	Cowardice, meekness, timidity.
Valuable	x	Invaluable, worthless, valueless.
Value	x	Disvalue, deficiency, inferiority.
Vanish	x	Appear, arrive, solidify.
Vanish	x	Appear, arrive, emerge.
Vanity	x	Modesty, humility, humbleness.
Vanquish	x	Discharge, yield, surrender.
Vapid	x	Lively, exciting, adequate.
Vapor	x	Dryness, belittle, diminish.
Variable	x	Constant, invariable, unstable.
Variably	x	Invariably, equal, certain.
Variance	x	Harmony, agreement, accord.
Variation	x	Fixation, stabilization, uniformity.
Varied	x	Similar, same, uniform.

Variegated	x	Unvaried, unspotted, solid.
Variety	x	Uniformity, homogeneity, similarity.
Various	x	Few, identical, uniform.
Varnish	x	Dullness, uncover, expose.
Vary	x	Preserve, fix, conform, harmonize.
Vast	x	Small, limited, insignificant.
Vault	x	Allow, decrease, decline.
Vaunt	x	Conceal, regret, belittle.
Veer	x	Straiten, continue, stay.
Vegetarian	x	Non-vegetarian, predatory, raptorial.
Vegetate	x	Develop, improve, activate.
Vehemence	x	Ambiguity, calmness, apathy.
Vehement	x	Cool, guarded, apathetic.
Veil	x	Unveil, expose, disclose.
Velocity	x	Slowness, deliberation, resistance.
Venal	x	Ethical, honest, incorruptible.
Vend	x	Buy, purchase, subsidize.
Venerable	x	Dishonourable, unimpressive, modern.

Venerate	x	Dishonour, blaspheme, denounce.
Veneration	x	Irreverence, disrespect, contempt.
Vengeance	x	Forgiveness, pardon, remission.
Venial	x	Abominable, inexcusable, unpardonable.
Venom	x	Antidote, love, kindness.
Venomous	x	Nonvenomous, nontoxic, beneficial.
Vent	x	Closure, suppress, absorb.
Ventilated	x	Unventilated, close, suffocating.
Venture	x	Certainty, assurance, idleness.
Venturesome	x	Unadventurous, afraid, beneficial.
Veracious	x	Untrue, deceitful, dishonest.
Veracity	x	Falsehood, deception, roughness.
Verbal	x	Nonverbal, written, formal.
Verbose	x	Concise, succinct, brief.
Verbosity	x	Consciousness, brevity, briefness.
Verdict	x	Accusation, indecision, truth.
Verge	x	Center, core, inner.
Verified	x	Unverified, disprove, refute.

Verify	x	Contradict, disprove, contest.
Verisimilitude	x	Difference, impossibility, unlikelihood.
Veritable	x	Fake, unreal, counterfeit.
Verity	x	Falsehood, fallacy, deceit.
Vernal	x	Wintry, autumnal, brumal.
Versatile	x	Incapable, amateur, limited.
Versed	x	Unskilled, ignorant, inexperienced.
Version	x	Text, problem, misinterpretation.
Vertical	x	Flat, horizontal, inclined.
Veteran	x	Novice, unskilled, amateur.
Veto	x	Support, allow, approve.
Vex	x	Amuse, appease, please.
Vexation	x	Pleasure, delight, happiness.
Vibrate	x	Steady, stay, remain.
Vice	x	Virtue, merit, righteousness.
Vicinity	x	Distance, remoteness, faraway.
Vicious	x	Virtuous, decent, ethical.
Vicissitude	x	Fixity, stability, uniformity.

Victim	x	Offender, culprit, defamer.
Victor	x	Loser, quitter, failure.
Victorious	x	Defeated, unsuccessful, conquered.
Victory	x	Defeat, disaster, collapse.
View	x	Blindness, reality, misconception.
Vigilance	x	Remissness, indifference, unwariness.
Vigilant	x	Remiss, negligent, inattentive.
Vigorous	x	Inanimate, delicate, inactive.
Vile	x	Worthy, noble, agreeable.
Villain	x	Hero, innocent, angel.
Villainous	x	Decent, honourable, virtuous.
Vindicate	x	Refute, accuse, condemn.
Vindictive	x	Forgiving, sympathetic, merciful.
Violate	x	Observe, comply, value.
Violence	x	Nonviolence, calmness, mildness.
Violent	x	Nonviolent, calm, composed.
Virgin	x	Blemished, polluted, inhabited.
Virile	x	Effeminate, impotent, unmanly.

Virtual	x	Actual, unrealistic, authentic.
Virtue	x	Vice, blemish, impurity.
Virtuous	x	Wicked, bad, dishonest.
Virulence	x	Calm, civility, diplomacy.
Visible	x	Invisible, unseen, sightless.
Vision	x	Actuality, reality, blindness.
Visionary	x	Tangible, actual, realistic.
Vital	x	Insignificant, unwanted, secondary.
Vitiate	x	Refine, cleanse, uplift.
Vivacious	x	Inanimate, constrained, spiritless.
Vivid	x	Dim, unclear, vague.
Viviparous	x	Oviparous, broody, ovoviviparous.
Vocation	x	Avocation, hobby, amusement.
Vociferous	x	Silent, noiseless, calm.
Vogue	x	Unfashionable, unpopular, anonymous.
Voice	x	Devoice, silence, quiet.
Void	x	Full, furnished, adequate.
Volatile	x	Certain, constant, definite.

Volition	x	Aversion, coercion, rejection.
Voluble	x	Un talkative, quiet, silent.
Volume	x	Minuteness, atom, crumb.
Voluntary	x	Compulsory, involuntary, forced.
Volunteer	x	Compulsory, enforced, mandatory.
Voluptuous	x	Abstinent, harsh, painful.
Voracious	x	Content, satisfied, uneager.
Votary	x	Opponent, defector, traitor.
Vouch	x	Break, condemn, contradict.
Vouchsafe	x	Deny, refuse, reject.
Vulgar	x	Refine, noble, appropriate.
Vulnerable	x	Invulnerable, guarded, protected

W

Waft	x	Keep, hold, calm.
Wail	x	Laugh, cheer, acclaim.
Wait	x	Act, haste, dispatch.
Waive	x	Approve, refuse, claim.
Wake	x	Sleep, hypnotize, lull.
Wakeful	x	Sleepy, drowsy, unaware.
Walk	x	Halt, ride, drive.
Wan	x	Blushing, blooming, lively.
Wander	x	Settle, remain, stay.
Wane	x	Thrive, brighten, increase.
Want	x	Abundance, adequacy, supplement.
Wanton	x	Chaste, decent, frigid.
War	x	Peace, accord, truce.

Ward	x	Aggression, assault, betray.
Warfare	x	Ceasefire, truce, concord.
Warlike	x	Peaceful, nonaggressive, amicable.
Warm	x	Cool, dispassionate, composed.
Warmth	x	Coolness, indifference, apathy.
Warn	x	Ignore, discourage, imperil.
Warrant	x	Denial, prohibition, rejection.
Wary	x	Unwary, incautious, careless.
Wash	x	Soil, pollute, contaminate.
Waste	x	Conserve, fertile, restoration.
Wasteful	x	Careful, economical, conserving.
Watch	x	Disregard, dismiss, ignore.
Watchful	x	Inattentive, careless, heedless.
Waver	x	Decide, advance, continue.
Wavering	x	Steady, decision, determination.
Wavy	x	Straight, even, plain.
Wax	x	Wane, abridge, decline.
Way	x	Deviation, barely, hardly.

Wayward	x	Amenable, obedient, controllable.
Weak	x	Strong, mighty, powerful.
Weaken	x	Strengthen, empower, augment.
Weakness	x	Strength, advantage, merit.
Weal	x	Woe, misery, suffering.
Wealth	x	Poverty, debt, deficiency.
Wear	x	Activate, abandon, renovate.
Weariness	x	Strength, vigor, energy.
Wearisome	x	Refreshing, amazing, absorbing.
Weary	x	Spirited, unwearied, energetic.
Weave	x	Unweave, untwist, separate.
Wed	x	Separate, divorce, disconnect.
Wedlock	x	Disunion, celibacy, separation.
Weep	x	Laugh, surge, stream.
Weight	x	Lightness, insignificance, advantage.
Weighty	x	Light, easy, unencumbered.
Welcome	x	Farewell, unwelcome, disagreeable.
Weld	x	Break, disconnect, separate.

Welfare	x	Misery, suffering, disadvantage.
Well	x	Unwell, diseased, ailing.
Wet	x	Dry, unsentimental, unadulterated.
Wheedle	x	Disenchant, offend, tease.
Whimper	x	Bang, acclaim, approval.
Whimsical	x	Normal, equable, steady.
White	x	Black, colorful, adverse.
Whole	x	Part, imperfect, scattered.
Wholesome	x	Noxious, unhealthy, contaminated.
Wholly	x	Partially, imperfectly, incompletely.
Wicked	x	Righteous, decent, noble, harmless.
Wickedness	x	Goodness, morality, righteousness.
Wide	x	Narrow, contracted, limited.
Widen	x	Shorten, curtail, shorten.
Wild	x	Tamed, civilized, inhabited.
Will	x	Indecision, compulsion, indulgence.
Willful	x	Unwilling, obedient, accidental.
Willing	x	Reluctant, disinclined, averse.

Win	x	Lose, defeat, upset.
Wind	x	Unwind, straighten, untwist.
Winding	x	Straight, direct, unwinding.
Winged	x	Wingless, apteral, slow.
Winner	x	Loser, quitter, failure.
Winning	x	Loosing, unsuccessful, unloved.
Winsome	x	Repulsive, unloved, displeasing.
Wisdom	x	Ignorance, imprudence, stupidity.
Wise	x	Foolish, unwise, irrational.
Wish	x	Dislike, resent, begrudge.
Wit	x	Seriousness, imprudence, stupidity.
Witchery	x	Reality, science, repulsion.
With	x	Without, against, alienated.
Withdraw	x	Propose, stay, advance.
Wither	x	Prosper, revive, thrive.
Withhold	x	Give up, release, abandon.
Within	x	Without, exterior, boarder.
Without	x	Within, inside, including.

Withstand	x	Yield, concede, surrender.
Witness	x	Disproof, refutation, participation.
Witty	x	Serious, unfunny, witless.
Woe	x	Joy, bliss, advantage.
Woeful	x	Joyous, cheerful, blessed.
Womanhood	x	Manhood, manliness, masculinity.
Womanly	x	Manly, unwomanly, strong.
Wonder	x	Certainty, disregard, apathy.
Wonderful	x	Unimpressive, familiar, expected.
Wonted	x	Exceptional, unusual, uncommon.
Word	x	Deed, silence, idea.
Work	x	Leisure, unemployment, idleness.
Workman	x	Employer, inspector, supervisor.
World	x	Void, nothingness, hair.
Worldly	x	Spiritual, unworldly, heavenly.
Worry	x	Comfort, calmness, unconcern.
Worse	x	Better, beneficial, useful.
Worship	x	Condemnation, dislike, censure.

Worth	x	Worthlessness, cheapness, futility.
Worthless	x	Worthy, valuable, excellent.
Worthy	x	Worthless, valueless, defective.
Wound	x	Heal, happiness, comfort.
Wrap	x	Unwrap, unwind, bare.
Wrath	x	Calmness, patience, pleasure.
Wrathful	x	Delighted, pleased, obliging.
Wreck	x	Rescue, conservation, construction.
Wrench	x	Straighten, untwist, heave.
Wretched	x	Admirable, blessed, excellent.
Written	x	Unwritten, oral, verbal.
Wrong	x	Right, accurate, perfect.
Wrought	x	Unformed, rough, crude.
Wry	x	Straight, direct, humorless.

X

Xenophobia   x   Fairness, impartiality, goodwill.

Y

Yawn	x	Close, conceal, blast.
Yearly	x	Perennial, everlasting, periodical.
Yearn	x	Loathe, refuse, hate.
Yell	x	Mumble, silence, whisper.
Yes	x	No, scarcely, disagreed.
Yesterday	x	Tomorrow, future, hereafter.
Yield	x	Resist, charge, resist.
Yielding	x	Unyielding, defiant, resisting.
Yoke	x	Freedom, liberty, emancipation.
Young	x	Old, mature, experienced.
Youth	x	Adulthood, majority, winter.
Youthful	x	Senile, adult, mature.

Z

Zeal	x	Apathy, indifference, coldness.
Zealot	x	Conservative, moderate, nonmilitant.
Zealous	x	Apathetic, cold, dispassionate.
Zenith	x	Nadir, base, unimportant.
Zero	x	Chief, apex, zenith.
Zest	x	Insipidity, apathy, blandness.
Zone	x	Whole, sphere, universe.

www.ingramcontent.com/pod-product-compliance
Lightning Source LLC
Chambersburg PA
CBHW051435250726
48655CB00001B/74